CASTRO, THE KREMLIN, AND
COMMUNISM IN LATIN AMERICA

Studies in Internatio

nelson P. Valdés
July 1969

Studies in International Affairs Number 9

CASTRO, THE KREMLIN, AND COMMUNISM IN LATIN AMERICA

by D. Bruce Jackson

The Washington Center of Foreign Policy Research
School of Advanced International Studies
The Johns Hopkins University

The Johns Hopkins Press, Baltimore

FOREWORD

In American eyes the cold war has been princi-
pally a struggle to contain Soviet expansionism. At
the outset, international communism was regarded
as an instrument of Soviet policy. As the differences
between Moscow and foreign communist parties and
states became manifest—most markedly in the case
of China—the meaning of international communism
and its relationship to Soviet power and policy became impossible to comprehend in terms of the old
categories of analysis. From the standpoint of its
impact on the cold war—or what remains of it—the
growing heterogeneity of communism in the third
world is particularly significant because it is there,
presumably, that the greatest opportunities for communist expansion lie.

It remains to be seen whether the special national,
social, and political positions of communist parties
and states in the third world will help or hinder them
from gaining power. What can be seen already is
that this separatism has sharpened some old dilemmas that confront the Soviet Union in trying to
harmonize its position as a great power with the
local interests and aspirations of independent communist states and parties.

Its dilemmas in Latin America are particularly
ironic because, except for China, Cuba is the only
noncommunist state since World War II to undergo
a successful communist revolution. And although
Castro's achievement owed nothing to Soviet help,
he conspicuously aligned Cuba with Moscow. Yet,

since that transformation, the differences between Cuban and Soviet interests and policies in Latin America have become substantial. And these differences are complicated by the Latin new left—by the rise of romantic revolutionary groups that have no affinity with the old-line communist parties in the area.

Mr. Jackson provides a rare insight into the contradictions and subtleties of the resulting relationship between Moscow, Havana, Latin American governments, communist parties, and revolutionary groups. By illuminating the confluence of these elements in Venezuela he shows us a cross section of international communism in a phase of international politics that scarcely resembles the familiar image of the cold war.

July 1968   Robert E. Osgood
                              Director
                              Washington Center of
                              Foreign Policy Research

CONTENTS

CASTRO, THE KREMLIN, AND COMMUNISM IN LATIN AMERICA

Studies in International Affairs Number 9

I. INTRODUCTION

Nowhere in international politics has the generation gap been more apparent than in the relations between Moscow's colorless post-Khrushchevian leaders and Havana's bearded angry young man, Fidel Castro. The world of the former is carefully structured, bureaucratic, and bound by tradition and vested interest to a rather inflexible system of communist parties more noted for discipline than revolutionary élan. The world of the latter, despite Castro's accession to the communist camp, has been a loose, leader-oriented aggregation of Latin American radicals more noted for revolutionary zeal than for discipline. In a very real sense, the Cuban-Soviet relationship of recent years has been between the irresponsibility, impatience, and rebelliousness of youth and the caution, shrewdness, and patience of middle age.

But the Cuban revolution has grown older. It has tasted both fruits of its own irresponsibility and bitter consequences of the shrewd maneuverings of its elders. The story of Soviet-Cuban differences over Latin American strategy from 1964 to 1967 is very much a story of the coming of age of "Fidelismo" in the world communist movement. Castro had always felt a certain contempt for the traditional Latin American communist parties and their Soviet mentor, and his experiences once he gained power in Cuba gave him little reason to change his outlook. As he began his attempts to foster similar revolutions in other parts of Latin America, he had little inclination to turn to the established communist parties, which, like the Cuban Communist Party (PSP), had been ineffective for over forty years. Instead, he gave his support to the leftist insurrectionary groups modeled on his own which were springing up outside the communist parties in much of the hemisphere.

Increasingly after 1961, however, Cuban economic survival and military security depended on Moscow, and Castro could not be entirely certain how much misbehavior the Soviets would tolerate and still foot the bill for his languishing economy. His own security thus depended, to some extent, on the degree to which he was willing to accept Soviet orthodoxy in both internal and external matters. The pressures for orthodoxy were greatest when Castro was least able to interpret the Soviet attitude toward him. This uncertainty reached its last major peak immediately following the overthrow of Khrushchev in late 1964, and in this period Castro consented to agreements with Moscow and the Latin American communist parties which compromised his previous independent posture in the world communist movement. Not only did Cuban representatives start appearing regularly at Soviet-sponsored international gatherings, but Havana and Peking began trading increasingly open insults. In addition, certain revolutionary leftists in Latin America began charging Fidel with having sold out to "revisionism," and Soviet nemesis Che Guevara disappeared mysteriously from the Cuban scene.

Whether Castro was really convinced that the new Soviet leaders were prepared to meet him halfway in return for his concessions remains uncertain. The indications are that he was at least partially

convinced of the righteousness of their behavior
vis-à-vis the Chinese and of their greater willingness
(as compared to Khrushchev) to meet their "fraternal obligations" to "liberation struggles" such as
those in Vietnam and Venezuela. It also appears that
for a time Castro was willing to give the established
communist parties a chance to prove their revolutionary militancy by cutting back his direct support
to competing leftist groups.

As 1965 drew to a close, however, Castro obviously
began to see things in a different perspective. His
November 1964 agreement with the communist parties of Latin America had endorsed Cuban-style
armed struggle in six Latin American countries, but
it had also asserted the right of each party to determine its own tactics. And it was this latter "right"
which the Latin American communist parties were
invoking to scuttle armed struggles in favor of less
blatantly extremist tactics. Moscow, in turn, seemed
to Castro to be much more concerned with outpoint-
ing the Chinese in the "Byzantine" battles of the
Sino-Soviet polemic than in actually stepping up aid
to world revolution.

More importantly, however, Castro was developing a feel for his position vis-à-vis the new Soviet
leaders, and he realized that they were just as inex-
tricably bound to support Cuba as Khrushchev had
been. Indeed, he may well have judged them even
more committed, for they had given top priority in
their foreign policy to restoring the "unity and cohesion of the socialist camp." Castro quite evidently
realized that Soviet attempts to isolate the Chinese
by being ostentatiously more "reasonable" placed
Moscow in no position to enforce orthodoxy. He,
on the other hand, could use some of the trappings

of orthodoxy to gain increased freedom of maneuver from Moscow. Thus it was that he gave the Cuban ruling party the orthodox name of the "Cuban Communist Party" at the same time that he was reorganizing it to deprive the old-line Cuban communists of any meaningful power. Thus it was also that he began the preparations for the Tricontinent Conference of January 1966 in apparent coordination with Moscow, but wound up by helping to push the conference into a repudiation of the Moscow line and a bypassing of the traditional communist parties in Latin America.

The Tricontinent Conference provided Castro with both the inspiration and the pretext for a renewal of his cultivation of revolutionary groups outside the Latin American communist parties. Instead of following Moscow's lead and treating the Tricontinent as another "front" conference whose decisions were useful propaganda and little more, Castro insisted that this had been an epoch-making event, by implication superseding the 1964 conference of Latin American communists which had bound him to dealing only through pro-Moscow parties. The significance of the conference to Castro was not merely practical, although it did give him an international organization which he could dominate and manipulate to his own ends. It also symbolized Castroism in the international sphere: the stress on action before ideology, on bravery before discipline, and on international aid to revolutionaries before construction of the comfortable society at home.

In the year following the Tricontinent Conference, Castro treated every criticism of the conference as a direct affront to the Cuban revolution. The Cuban press launched a tirade against the

Yugoslavs for publishing articles critical of the Tricontinent Conference; there was oblique Cuban criticism of Soviet attempts to disavow the interventionist implications of the Havana meeting; and at international communist front gatherings, Cuban representatives protested the lack of attention paid to the Tricontinent movement. Finally, joining hands with two other "hungry" members of the communist camp, North Korea and North Vietnam, Castro began an attempt to establish a permanent fraction within the communist movement. This was to be a grouping which could not be discredited with a Chinese label but which would act as a continuing pressure group to prod the European communist governments into greater revolutionary efforts in the third world and a harder line towards the U.S.

On the ideological plane, the Cuban doctrine became increasingly explicit in its criticism of the traditional behavior of Latin American communists and in its derogation of the standard Soviet answers to the problem of Latin American revolution. The culmination of this trend was reached in early 1967. The Cuban government published a major treatise on the question of Latin American revolution which rejected Soviet formulas, and Fidel Castro stated openly that he would ignore questions of affiliation with the world communist movement in his dealings with Latin American revolutionaries.

Where two years previously Castro had seemed insecure and utterly tied to the firm policies of a no-nonsense Soviet leadership, now he was ostentatiously confident of his ability to twist the Soviet tail and get away with it. When Latin American communists would call for observance of the November 1964 agreements which forbade Cuban interference with their internal affairs, Castro would call for loyalty to the Tricontinent Conference and to the Latin American revolution. And the Soviets, while obviously favoring the traditional parties, were still apparently unwilling or unable to take measures strong enough to put Castro in his place.

The place of the Venezuelan revolutionary movement in this evolution was a critical one. When the Latin American communists meeting in Havana in November 1964 pledged support to "freedom fighters" in six countries as part of their bargain with Cuba, Venezuela was uppermost in everyone's mind. When pro-Soviet communists began talking about using "broad united front" tactics rather than narrow partisan warfare, it was in Venezuela that their arguments had their most obvious application. It was the Venezuelan Communist Party which first threw the 1964 agreements into question by trying to reverse a previous commitment to armed struggle. It was the role played at the Tricontinent Conference by the dissident wing of the Venezuelan "Armed Forces of National Liberation" (FALN) which prompted the Cuban-Yugoslav polemics over the conference. It was the struggle of the Venezuelan FALN dissidents to maintain the guerrilla insurgency against the "liquidationist" attempts of the traditional communist party which provided the pretext, if not the inspiration, for the new surge of Cuban involvement in the doctrinal battles of Latin American revolutionaries. Finally, it may have been Castro's realization that the Soviets were prepared to establish diplomatic relations with the Venezuelan government which convinced him of the urgency of securing an independent position in the communist world and doing his utmost to sustain existing guerrilla movements in Latin America. In any case, it is in Venezuela that the Cuban-Soviet conflict in outlook and interests has emerged in its clearest outlines.

II. THE HISTORICAL SETTING

Legacy of the Comintern

The current Soviet-Cuban differences over Latin American revolutionary strategy have roots as deep as the Latin American communist parties themselves, most of which had their genesis prior to 1930. The parties were by no means a homogeneous grouping, but they were all distinguished by one unique and important characteristic: Like other members of the Comintern, they were more servants of Soviet policy than agents of revolution. Although Soviet policy was by definition "revolutionary," its revolutionary content was restricted by the primary policy goal of the U.S.S.R. to build and defend Soviet socialism. If the Comintern line was "soft," the communist parties would befriend groups previously denounced as traitors to the revolution. If the line was "hard," as it was from 1928–34, then the communist parties were obliged to take positions of such uncompromising militancy that they lost virtually all their popular support.

In Latin American communism, the legacy of the Comintern rigidities was particularly pronounced, for no part of the world except perhaps colonial Africa was farther from Soviet interests in this period. In addition, perhaps because of a basic conflict between communist discipline and Latin American *personalismo*, the leaders who emerged within the framework of the established communist parties were never possessed of the charisma needed to make them the Uncle Ho's or Chairman Mao's of their countries. Orthodoxy rather than audacity, and shrewdness rather than breadth of vision were the characteristics rewarded by their system. Thus, while political influence was always to be won for the price of the steady subsidy given by Moscow,[1] political power was never to be won. Relative influence and reliable discipline made the communists useful allies of other political groupings, but they rarely became more than that.

The chief corollaries of the relationship of the Latin American communist parties to Moscow were two mutually reinforcing characteristics, "opportunism" and a sense of "geographic fatalism." Geography alone told the communists that a victorious revolution in Latin America would face a much more formidable foe in the U.S. and a much less reliable friend in the U.S.S.R. than would one in Asia or Central Europe. To start with, then, a modicum of influence was a more rewarding goal than total power. But in addition, the regular Soviet dole was a steady force pushing the parties toward short-run gains at the expense of long-range strategy. Soviet funding depended not merely on a party's prospects for gaining power but also on its success in generating useful propaganda and demonstrations and on its ability to influence the government in power to adopt positions favorable to Soviet foreign policy goals.

But if the structure of the Comintern (later Cominform) relationship inclined the Latin American parties toward opportunism, their own inclinations reinforced the tendency. Many of the Latin American communist parties carved out moderately comfortable niches for themselves on the left fringes of Latin American societies—sometimes legal, sometimes illegal but tolerated—from which they could join in the normal political bargaining of the countries concerned. Once engaged in this pleasant pursuit, the communist leaders (many of whom by the late 1940's had served periods in the government or congress) tended to show little interest in the possibilities of revolution by other tactics. The success of Mao's revolutionary strategy in China, for example, made no marked impact on the thinking of Latin American communists.

In the early postwar years, the one example in which communists played a substantial role in the national politics of a Latin American country merely buttressed this opportunism with geographical fatalism. In Guatemala under Arbenz the communists came closer to power than ever before, but they were also decisively thwarted by forces backed by the U.S. The lessons seemed to be the familiar ones: opportunistic alliances with "national bourgeois" political forces are rewarding vehicles for political influence, but the geographic position of Latin America precludes total communist victory.

Competition on the Left

A natural consequence of this behavior by the communist parties was the growth of a welter of other parties and revolutionary groupings on the far left, some as a result of splits in existing communist parties, others of independent origin. Indeed, the Chinese communist deviation had less impact in Latin America than elsewhere in part because Latin

American communism had never successfully dealt with the previous "left deviation" of Trotskyism.

Trotskyism did not exactly thrive in Latin America, but the behavior of the established communist parties gave frequent support to Trotsky's thesis that Stalin had sacrificed world revolution for the sake of "socialist construction" in the U.S.S.R. Trotskyite theories were thus able to maintain a significant following of leftist revolutionaries who found the traditional communist parties too opportunistic and too slow to fire the starting guns of revolution. Trotskyite influence was predictably strongest in those countries where the traditional communists were most fully reconciled to working for limited goals within accepted rules of the national political game, as in Argentina, Uruguay, Mexico, and Cuba. There seems little doubt that the number two man in Castro's revolutionary movement, Che Guevara, was at least partly influenced by Trotskyite ideas, and he was claimed as a friend by Trotskyites in Cuba and the rest of Latin America.[2]

By the time of Castro's "invasion" of Cuba from Mexico in December 1956, the communist parties of Cuba and the rest of Latin America were fully accustomed to dealing with ultrarevolutionary movements arising on their left and were understandably suspicious of all of them, including Castro's. Most activities of such groups fell into the category of "putschism," hopeless and short-lived insurrections whose main effect was to provoke the authorities into incarcerating all available revolutionaries. The communists often were the most available. Castro's attack on the Moncada military barracks in 1953 had certainly fallen into that category, however influential his subsequent speech, "History Will Absolve Me," may have been.

Impact of the Cuban Revolution

The success of Castro's revolution and its rapid conversion into a communist revolution presented the Latin American communists with a rather difficult doctrinal problem. The events themselves could be easily explained in conventional communist terms: The communists first allied themselves with a "bourgeois-democratic" movement which threw out the old order; then the communists threw out the bourgeois-democrats to accomplish the second stage of the revolution. But the role of Fidel Castro, who was both Kerensky and Lenin to the Cuban revolution, was not so easily defined. After serving as a bourgeois-democrat in the first stage of the revolution, Fidel joined, nay led, the communists in throwing his erstwhile class brethren out. This called for a bit of semantic juggling (it took until 1963 for Soviet theoreticians to agree on the proper term for a Castro-style changeling: "revolutionary democrat"), but it obviously fell within the general scope of approved revolutionary models. The real problem was Castro's implicit challenge to the doctrine of geographic fatalism and his explicit urging that other revolutionaries in the hemisphere duplicate his feat.

At first, these doctrinal problems were brushed aside in the enthusiasm of the moment. Proof of the onward march of communism into Latin America was now, after all, manifest. The Soviets had clearly not expected Castro to declare himself a communist quite so quickly, nor could they estimate the economic burden which the Cuban economy would present for them, but these were only vague quibbles at that point. The Cuban revolution provided a strong, if short-lived, boost to the waning ideological fervor of the Soviet party. In addition, it came fast on the heels of a major Soviet breakthrough in the technology of war which altered substantially the East-West power balance in areas distant from Soviet borders. If the Soviet ICBM's could deliver a convincing nuclear threat most of the way round the world, where did that leave the doctrine of geographic fatalism?

Whether or not the Soviets had allowed themselves to be convinced by their own propaganda on the largely mythical "end to U.S. military superiority," they did evidently feel a new surge of optimism. At least some Soviet leaders had become convinced that there was a definite tide in world events which could be taken at the flood with bold initiatives to produce a new round of socialist victories. In the Congo in 1960, Khrushchev embarked on a risky gamble of direct involvement with a promising but not yet established revolutionary nationalist movement. And in Latin America, particularly after the Bay of Pigs episode had indicated that the precedent of Guatemala in 1954 was no longer valid, the Soviets seemed willing to listen to Castro's claims that his revolution could be exported. For a brief period there were even signs that they had adopted the Castroite estimate of the potential value of guerrilla tactics.[3]

Although Soviet leaders were willing to agree that things had changed with the Cuban revolution, several factors kept them from wholly accepting the Castroite theory of how the revolution had come about, with all its implications for the rest of the Latin American communist movement. They still considered Castro's tactics to have been adventuristic and suspected that they would not have succeeded if Batista's dictatorship had not already been on the verge of collapse. For a movement identified by the public as democratic, Castro's tactics may initially have made sense, but the negative aspects of these tactics were multiplied by Castro's increasing identification with the communist camp. A reorganized communist movement could not use them and gain even a fraction of the popular support Castro had enjoyed. A democratic reformer could not use them without becoming tainted by Castro's sellout to communism.

Latin American Communist Reactions

Moscow's willingness to assist Castro in his efforts to spread his brand of revolution in Latin America did not extend to pressuring the Latin American communist parties to adopt his tactics. Indeed, one of the major points of dissension between Moscow and Peking was the Soviet claim that "peaceful transition to socialism" was now possible. Moscow was asserting that in view of the "growing strength of the socialist camp," the opportunist tactics used by communists such as those of Latin America might not produce such limited results after all, but might lead all the way to "scientific socialism." The success of the Cuban communists' alliance with Castro provided one of the best and perhaps the only demonstration of their thesis.

The established communist parties of Latin America, therefore, managed for the most part to avoid any searching reappraisals of their policies and tactics. Almost all were able to reaffirm existing policies after paying appropriate homage to the Cuban revolution. The main counterpressures came from other leftist parties and from youth wings of the established parties, where Castro's heroic posture and apparent shortcut to revolution had evoked the strongest emotional response.

The Venezuelan example. Castroite pressures on the communist party were strongest, ironically, not in a country where Cuban theory could easily claim that revolutionary conditions were ready to be brought to a head with guerrilla warfare, but in Venezuela, where the government in power was popular, democratic, and effective. Cuban theory, as expressed by Che Guevara in *Guerrilla Warfare*, had stated explicitly that these were precisely the conditions under which guerrilla tactics could *not* succeed: "Where a government has come into power through some form of popular vote, fraudulent or not, and maintains at least an appearance of constitutional legality, the guerrilla outbreak cannot be promoted, since the possibilities of peaceful struggle have not yet been exhausted" (p. 16).

Subsequent events have shown that Che Guevara was quite right on this question, but by the time Castro was becoming fully and publicly identified with the world communist movement in late 1961, it was clear that theory could not be the deciding factor in keeping Castroism alive in the hemisphere. Cuban attempts in 1959 to export revolution against the targets called for by theory—the "reactionary" governments of the Dominican Republic, Haiti, Nicaragua, Panama, and Paraguay—had met total failure. Furthermore, as Castro's claims to being the only true reformer in Latin America began to be increasingly threatened by his own subservience to Moscow and by U.S. support of democratic reforms under the Alliance for Progress, the target of Cuban anger shifted from dictatorships to democratic reformists. It became much more important to Castro to discredit reformist regimes— either by provoking military coups or by forcing reformist leaders to undertake repressive actions against leftists—than to work seriously for the overthrow of right-wing dictatorships. And guerrilla action seemed to guarantee either military coups or reformist complicity in military repressions, both of which would hinder effective popular reform and tarnish the democratic image of Castro's competitors.

The conditions which made guerrilla warfare possible in Venezuela were both political and physical. Physically, the Venezuelan terrain is sufficiently rugged and the vegetation sufficiently impenetrable that guerrillas, bandits, or anyone else willing to endure the rigors of the jungle can evade authorities almost indefinitely. In addition, the 1,400-mile Venezuelan coastline makes access to and from Cuba by sea possible with only a moderate risk of detection. Politically, the key ingredients were the presence in Venezuela of a large contingent of Fidelista youth anxious to strike heroic blows for the revolution and the existence of substantial sectors within the established political parties which felt that their own political fortunes could be advanced by confronting President Betancourt with a guerrilla problem. Assisting these factors were the institutional vacuum and the strong public acceptance of violence which followed the 1958 overthrow of the Pérez Jiménez military dictatorship.

In 1960, the left wing of Betancourt's government party, *Acción Democrática* (AD), had broken away to form a Castroite opposition party, the MIR (*Movimiento de Izquierda Revolucionaria*). The MIR was joined in vehement opposition to Betancourt by leftist elements of the principal Venezuelan opposition party, the URD. Together they constituted an attractive set of allies for the Venezuelan Communist Party (PCV), which joined them in establishing the Venezuelan "National Liberation Front" (FLN). It was in this context that the Venezuelan armed struggle gradually began during 1961 and 1962. It was clearly not in any sense a gratuitous decision of the communist party to use Castroite tactics and then to enlist as many allies as possible in the effort. It was rather a case of alliance politics leaving the communist party no choice but to endorse Castroite tactics if it did not wish to lose both its allies and its claims to leadership of the "liberation struggle." Added to this were PCV resentment and frustration at being totally excluded from the fruits of government after assisting in the overthrow of Pérez Jiménez.

The decision of the PCV to commit itself to an armed struggle against Betancourt, reached finally at a PCV plenum in December 1962, was the result of a lengthy intra-party debate. The Third Congress of the PCV in March 1961 had been ambiguous about the form of struggle to be used, calling for the usual "mastery of all forms of struggle." But it also asserted that to carry out revolutionary transformations without bloodshed ". . . is no more than a remote possibility" in view of the

character of the enemy.[4] Following the Third Congress, the party prepared for armed struggle while
conducting what one spokesman termed euphe-
mistically a "fertile discussion" on means of attaining power.[5] The terms of this debate have never
been made public, even in the recent Cuban airings
of PCV dirty linen. The reason for this omission
may well be that a major deciding factor in the debate was the matter of outside finances. In any
event, within two months after the debate was
definitively resolved at the fifth PCV plenum, the
communists and their allies organized an "Armed
Forces of National Liberation" (FALN) and
launched a well-financed campaign of urban terrorism and rural guerrilla warfare.

All available evidence indicates that Cuba was a
key outside factor in the resolution of the PCV line.
Aside from the obvious responsiveness of the FALN
to propaganda emanating from Havana and the dis-
covery of a Cuban arms shipment on the Venezuelan
coast in November, 1963, there was the independent
behavior of the PCV leadership, which could not
be explained by an internal power shift in the ruling party organs. Gustavo Machado and Jesus Faria,
long considered on the Moscow side of any internal
PCV debates, remained in the key party positions,
yet beginning at the East German party congress
in January 1963, the Venezuelans joined the Cubans
in a neutral stance on the question of condemning
the Chinese communists.[6] For some time thereafter,
Castro and the PCV were the closest of allies, and
Soviet policy toward the PCV could not be mean-
ingfully discussed except in terms of Soviet-Cuban
or Soviet-Cuban-Chinese relations.

The Missile Crisis and Its Reverberations

Almost paradoxically, the shift of the Venezuelan Communist Party took place at almost the same time that the Soviets were retreating toward a more cautious foreign policy line as a result of the Cuban missile crisis. A consequence of the installation and withdrawal of missiles in Cuba was the loss of Soviet interest and assets for bold maneuvering in Latin America. The Soviets could no longer entertain illusions concerning the U.S. willingness to act forcefully to protect its interests in the hemisphere. In addition, they had compromised the two assets which had made them attractive to Latin American nationalists: distance and power. With the installation of missiles, the image of the U.S.S.R. as a power too remote to represent an imperialistic threat was shattered; with their removal, the image of the U.S.S.R. as an effective foil against the U.S. was also destroyed.

But if communist expectations in Latin America were sharply lowered as a result of the missile crisis, there was no corresponding decline in the Soviet commitment to aid Latin American revolutionaries. To the contrary, the Soviet embarrassment had produced a situation in which clever revolutionaries could demand more assistance as the price of their continued allegiance to the U.S.S.R. in the Sino-Soviet dispute, and it was this tactic that the Cubans and Venezuelan communists began using in 1963. Castro traded friendly overtures with Peking and refused to sign the nuclear test-ban treaty; the PCV maintained a studied neutrality in the Sino-Soviet dispute, criticising neither and offering its "national liberation war" to both powers as a ready-made cause for proving their revolutionary *bona fides*.

Moscow in 1963 could do little but accept its role. After the missile crisis, Russia was on the defensive against both the United States and Red China and could not afford to make any moves regarding existing guerrilla wars which could be portrayed as a sellout of "national liberation struggles." Furthermore, Soviet propaganda had already pictured the Venezuelan government as being totally manipulated by Wall Street and the Pentagon. Moscow thus had no obvious opportunities at the Venezuelan government level which could be jeopardized by the armed struggle. Likewise, within the PCV, the pro-Moscow leadership remained at least nominally in charge and committed to armed struggle tactics. Finally, of course, acceptance of violent tactics by communists in Venezuela was useful proof to ideological fence-sitters such as Castro that Soviet talk of peaceful coexistence was not equivalent to abandoning support for revolutionary struggles.

Meanwhile, the Soviets and Cubans were engaged in continuous maneuvering and sparring, each seeking to get the most out of their increasingly expensive relationship. Prominent among the bargaining points was Castro's position vis-à-vis the rest of the world communist movement. Much of Castro's rage at the Soviets over the missile pullout had been vented on the Latin American communist parties. In a speech on January 16, 1963, Castro indirectly accused the traditional party leaders of spreading "false interpretations" of the Cuban revolution to justify their policy of "peaceful transition" and accused unidentified communists in the hemisphere of "conformism" with imperialism and "fear of revolutions." Castro's contempt for the traditional communists was made even more explicit in his talks with the French journalist, Claude Julien, which were published in *Le Monde* March 22 and 23, 1963. "What did the revolutionaries of Europe and America do [during the October crisis]?" asked Castro. "Only the Venezuelans reacted. But the big parties which call themselves revolutionary did not stir. They are not revolutionaries, they are bureaucrats, they are satellites."

Soviet reaction to these outbursts, characteristically, was not immediate, but the Latin American communists were seriously concerned that Castro's new mood might drag them into the quagmire of guerrilla warfare. In February 1963, the Brazilian communist leader, Luis Carlos Prestes, flew first to Moscow for talks and then to Havana. In an interview in Havana he stated bluntly: "There are persons who believe that the initiation of an armed struggle in Brazil to depose the government would constitute the best support for Cuba. In the present conditions of Brazil, this would be completely wrong."[7] Soon thereafter, and perhaps at the behest of Prestes and other Latin American communist leaders, Castro was invited to Moscow for some serious talk about this and other matters.

The public outcome of the Castro-Khrushchev talks was a joint communiqué, published on May 23, which contained a carefully worked out compromise formula on Latin American revolutions: ". . . the question of the peaceful or nonpeaceful road toward socialism in one country or another will be definitely decided by the struggling peoples themselves, according to the practical correlation of class forces and the degree of resistance of the exploiting classes to the socialist transformation of society."[8]

In other words, the Cubans were to cease their

attempts to dictate the policies of Latin American communists. That these words were an important victory for the traditional Latin American communist parties was made clear later in the year when the Chilean communist leader Luis Corvalán was able to quote from the Castro-Khrushchev communiqué to refute Chinese criticism of Chilean Communist Party tactics.[9]

The compromise was only a partial success, however. The Cubans moderated their line superficially to acknowledge the possibility of peaceful paths to power, but they renounced none of their basic positions and refused to join the traditional communist leaderships in moves against Chinese "deviations." The verbal hostilities between Castro and the traditional communist leaders of the hemisphere came to, at most, a temporary truce; no settlement was in sight. Indeed, as the months passed in 1964, it increasingly appeared that the Cubans felt bound to the line of the Castro-Khrushchev communiqué only to the degree that it remained expedient. By the time the election returns in Chile were made public in September, the dictates of expediency had apparently changed. With the victory of Eduardo Frei over the communist-backed Allende in Chile, the "peaceful way" had failed in Cuban eyes, while elsewhere a rise in world sugar prices had given the Cubans a heady feeling of independence from the strings of the Soviet dole. Thus in September 1964, Castro once again spoke out openly on the "inevitability" of armed struggle almost everywhere in Latin America.[10]

III. MOSCOW CHANGES TACTICS AND RULERS, 1964

Castro's drift back into his customary impudence during 1964 coincided, unbeknownst to him, with developments in the Soviet party Presidium which led, inter alia, to the removal from power of the Soviet leader who was closest in temperament to Castro, shoe-banging brinksman Premier Khrushchev. The extent to which the changing mood in Moscow affected Soviet policy before Khrushchev's ouster is difficult to gauge, but by late summer of 1964 there were signs of a search for new tactics to deal with some of the stickier messes in which Khrushchev's impulsive methods had entangled the U.S.S.R.

One of the stickiest of these was to be found in the international communist movement, where the Chinese deviation and Khrushchev's determination to defeat it in a head-on confrontation had allowed a variety of other unruly growths to develop. In Latin America, Castroism was exerting a disruptive influence on the communist movement out of proportion to Castro's declining prestige in Latin American society, and the traditional communist parties were in disarray after two serious setbacks. In Venezuela, a new president had been elected in a massive 94 percent voter turnout despite massive communist violence designed to disrupt the elections; in Brazil the increasingly leftist government of Goulart had been overthrown with little more than a whimper from the communists and their allies. The traditional communists of the hemisphere were demoralized and soon to become more so with the victory of Frei over Allende in Chile.

Theoretical Engagement

The first clear indication that the Soviets intended to do something about the Latin American communist movement came with the publication of two articles on Latin American themes in the July and August issues of the Soviet Communist Party theoretical journal *Kommunist*. As others have noted, such an occurrence was an unusual event in view of the *Kommunist's* usual emphasis on internal Soviet affairs. Herbert Dinerstein, in his 1966 study on Soviet policy in Latin America, concluded that the two articles signaled an important Soviet policy shift, in that armed struggle and guerrilla activity by communist parties were explicitly approved in an authoritative Soviet journal for the first time.[1] The second of the two articles in fact stated: "An analysis of recent events establishes that in countries where dictators are in power, [dictators] who are henchmen of foreign monopolies, the development of the struggle on a broad front, including armed struggle, and the creation of partisan detachments in some areas, is a completely justified course."[2]

This endorsement of violence was so phrased, however, as seemingly to exclude the one notable case in which guerrilla tactics had been used by a communist party. The sentence immediately following the above states that the tactics of partisan warfare ". . . cannot be mechanically transferred to countries where in the last few years the people have overthrown military-police dictatorships, where the governments coming to power on a wave of revolutionary developments have been forced . . . to liberalize the regime . . . where democratic and progressive organizations have emerged from the underground and begun overt political activities." This definition was obviously not merely designed to exclude liberal democracies in general. It is much more precise about where guerrilla warfare is unsuitable, and it pointedly suggests that Venezuela after the overthrow of Pérez Jiménez was one such place.

The chief significance of the *Kommunist* articles lay not in their meagre concessions to armed struggle, but in the new Soviet involvement which they represented, the new Soviet willingness to grapple with the problem of the Latin American parties. Foremost among these problems was that of "armed struggle" versus "mass struggle," and Moscow had finally shown itself willing to confront this question openly. It was in the atmosphere set by these articles and the Soviet attitudes they reflected that a meeting of all the Latin American communist parties was planned for late November 1964 in Havana.

Togliatti's Thesis and the Chinese Angle

The new flexibility and "reasonableness" in the Soviet attitude toward Latin American communism had little or no connection with the Soviet estimate of the prospects for revolution in Latin America. Nor was it traceable wholly to the then impending removal of Khrushchev. Khrushchev himself must have feared that he had entered a blind alley in attempting a new international communist conference before order had been attained even among pro-

Moscow communist parties of the world. And by the fall of 1964 there were influential voices in the Western communist world telling the Soviet leaders that new tactics were essential in the battle against the Chinese. The most dramatic of these was that of the Italian communist leader Palmiro Togliatti, who upon his death in August 1964 left an unpublished memorandum telling Khrushchev—and his successors—precisely how they should go about handling the Chinese problem.

The essence of Togliatti's advice was that the Chinese were most vulnerable when challenged on concrete problems and least vulnerable when challenged in theoretical generalities. Rather than pressing toward a confrontation with the Chinese at an international conference, advised Togliatti, the movement should ". . . proceed by groups of parties to a series of meetings for a profound examination and a better definition of the tasks presenting themselves today in the different sectors of our movement (Western Europe, Latin America . . .etc.)."[3] After enough of such regional conferences and bilateral discussions, the Chinese would be sufficiently isolated that an international conference might be possible or even (as Togliatti clearly hoped) unnecessary.

How far Khrushchev would have gone in the direction of Togliatti's advice remains speculative, but it certainly became much easier for the U.S.S.R. to follow this path after his overthrow in October. Not only did Brezhnev and Kosygin have a mandate for changing Khrushchev's policies toward the Chinese, they also had the important advantage of being little known quantities. Their carefully orchestrated efforts for 'world communist unity' could not be discredited automatically as Khrushchevian maneuvers, and the sincerity of their offers of "joint action" with the Chinese was not immediately suspect. An indication of the line they would follow was provided shortly after Khrushchev's ouster, when the Soviet newspaper *Pravda* published a favorable commentary on an Italian Communist Party plenum which had firmly endorsed the Togliatti memorandum.[4] Peking's charge that the Kremlin was now pursuing "Khrushchevism without Khrushchev" was not far from the mark, but with Khrushchev out of view some of his policies had a much better chance of success.

The departure of Khrushchev also gave Moscow a strong hand in dealing with Castro, who suddenly found himself dependent on a Soviet leadership lacking Khrushchev's personal commitment to Cuba. Whatever the assurances given to Castro by Khrushchev's successors, he must have realized that Brezhnev and Kosygin were not partners to verbal understandings he had reached with Khrushchev and that they had not endorsed their predecessor's blustering pronouncements at the U.N. over such matters as Cuban overflights. Indeed, Khrushchev's handling of Cuban matters was almost certainly a major aspect of the "hare-brained scheming" and unseemly behavior which had been among the pretexts for his ouster. Castro could only guess where he stood in the Brezhnev-Kosygin balance sheet of assets and liabilities, and presumably the Soviet leaders found it useful to keep him guessing as long as possible.

The 1964 Havana Conference

The facts surrounding the conference of twenty-two Latin American communist parties in Havana in late September 1964 have never been made entirely clear. The first indication that it had taken place came on January 19, 1965 with the publication of the conference communiqué in *Pravda*. Soviet publicity of the conference suggested that it had been called at the initiative of the Cubans or the Latin American communist parties or both. All the evidence, however, indicates that it involved primarily a Soviet initiative designed to drive a permanent wedge between Castro and the Chinese and to isolate Latin American communism from Chinese influence. Not only were the Soviets first to publish the communiqué of the conference (the Cubans followed a day later), but the conference itself followed perfectly the scheme previously suggested by Togliatti.

In any event, the November 1964 Havana conference was a milestone both in Cuban relations with the established Latin American communist parties and in Cuban relations with Peking. The conference brought Castro face-to-face with Moscow-line communist leaders from virtually all Latin American countries, and with no competing Castroite or pro-Chinese factions present as an alternative. As long as these communists evinced a willingness to make concessions to Cuban views, Castro could hardly refuse to cooperate. And concessions were in fact forthcoming, perhaps enough to convince Castro that the Soviets were sincere in wishing to revitalize the Latin American communist movement along more militant lines.

The conference communiqué indicated that in return for Cuban agreement to deal only with the established Latin American communist parties, the Soviets and their followers had conceded the necessity of supporting guerrilla warfare in several areas where local communists had previously judged the popular mood to be unready for armed struggle. The communiqué not only called for "support for freedom fighters" in the controversial case of Venezuela, but also in Guatemala, Honduras, Colombia, Paraguay, and Haiti. In other countries, the traditional communist parties might pursue their customary opportunism with renewed abandon, freed from the threat of Cuban-supported insurgencies on their left flank, but in these six, it seemed that Castro could exact a compensatory effort along more Fidelista lines.

For a brief period, events seemed to bear out this description of the Moscow-Havana compromise. Guerrilla insurgency in Venezuela was stepped up in early 1965; Colombian communists began voicing new support for the guerrilla bands in the hills; and a new guerrilla organization, the FAR (Rebel Armed Forces), made its appearance in Guatemala with the blessings of the local communist party. Elsewhere in the hemisphere, the Moscow-line parties were working to organize a "solidarity with Cuba" conference, apparently to fulfill a part of the Havana agreement which called for increased solidarity with the "embattled island." The Cubans, in turn, began to avoid general pronouncements on the inevitability of armed struggle in Latin America. Later in the year, they openly switched support from a dissident Castroite group in Guatemala to the guerrilla group sponsored by the local communist party.[5]

The Chinese reaction. These developments in the Latin American communist movements were overshadowed by a more dramatic development arising from the Havana conference: the development of a major schism between Havana and Peking. Just as Togliatti had foreseen, the act of convoking a regional meeting to dicuss "concrete situations" had resulted in a rejection of Chinese positions and a commitment to isolate Peking by means of general agreement on the need to ban all "factional activity." The Chinese reaction to the conference was immediate and vehement. Shortly after the conference, a delegation of Latin American communists headed by the Cuban Carlos Rafael Rodriguez left for Peking in an attempt to explain the soundness of the Havana accords. According to a Bolivian writer, they were denounced by Mao Tse-tung himself:

Mao Tse-tung had one of his rare attacks of fury and said that China would never accept the challenge launched by Castro, who in aiding the Venezuelans was seeking more the support of Moscow than of China. He added that of the three "demons" of the present world—imperialism, the atomic bomb, and revisionism—, Castro accepted the third because he was afraid of the first two. When a Uruguayan delegate tried to interrupt him, Mao told him that he was "speaking in the name of 650 million people," and he asked him how many he represented. He also had a violent exchange of words with the Cuban Carlos Rafael Rodriguez.[6]

It would appear from this report, as well as from Castro's admission in a speech on March 13 that he had been "naive," that the Cuban leader had seriously misjudged the intensity of Chinese feelings in the Sino-Soviet dispute. He must also have failed to recognize fully the anti-Chinese thrust behind the Soviet interest in the Havana conference. The mere fact that the Cubans bothered to send a delegation to tell the Chinese they had just been shut out of the hemisphere indicates a definite misjudgment. It appears that Castro partially believed that the promises extracted from Moscow for substantial material aid for the Venezuelan FALN and endorsement of several other Latin American guerrilla groups would persuade the Chinese to forego their separate interests in the hemisphere.

YEAR OF THE SOVIET-CUBAN TRUCE: 1965

The Cuban-Chinese Split

Castro's education in Sino-Soviet politics continued at an intensive pace as the new Soviet leadership pressed its advantage against the Chinese. As
Brezhnev and Kosygin's seeming willingness to make
concessions to the Chinese was met by Chinese
obstinacy, Castro found himself with no choice but
to side more and more with Moscow. Before the
reverberations of the 1964 Havana conference had
died down, Castro was being maneuvered toward
another Soviet-sponsored conference, the March
"preparatory meeting" for an eventual world communist conference. Again Brezhnev and Kosygin
had backed off so far from Khrushchev's position on
an international conference that Castro could find no
excuse not to be represented. Again the Chinese
would not accept his reasoning. An attempt to mollify the Chinese may have occurred in early February when Che Guevara interrupted his African tour
to visit Peking, where, according to the New China
News Agency, he was joined by two other high-
ranking Cubans sent from Havana.[1]
Neither Guevara's visit nor other attempts to pla-
cate the Chinese had any visible success. Castro was
clearly ready to wash his hands of the Chinese by
the time of the March 2 "preparatory meeting" in
Moscow, where he was represented by a high-rank-
ing delegation headed by his brother, Raul. On
March 12, Fidel Castro ended his long silence on

the Sino-Soviet split with a speech which clearly informed the Chinese that their caustic hints about flaws in his revolutionary integrity were both unwarranted and highly unwelcome in Cuba. The full text of this speech was published in *Pravda* on March 18, a rare honor for Castro. Thus began a period of unusual harmony between the Cubans and the Soviets, which lasted through most of 1965 and was clearly terminated only with the Tricontinent Conference of January 1966.

Guevara's Disappearance

The new Soviet-Cuban harmony was greatly helped by the absence of Che Guevara, who dropped from public view almost immediately after returning from his African tour in mid-March. Whatever Guevara's relationship to Castro at that time, his relinquishment of all positions of influence in the Cuban regime eliminated one of the major obstacles to Cuban-Soviet rapprochement. The coincidence was too striking to be accidental. Toward the end of Guevara's journey, his public statements had waxed increasingly critical of the U.S.S.R. and Eastern Europe, precisely at a time when Castro was lining up increasingly with the U.S.S.R. against the Chinese.[2] Guevara was also becoming more frank about difficulties and mistakes of the Cuban revolution, perhaps in a manner offensive to Castro. Latin American Trotskyites alleged during 1966 that Castro had liquidated Guevara on Soviet instructions as the quid pro quo of continued financial aid.[3] While this bit of speculation proved unfounded, it does seem plausible that Moscow demanded changes in the economic field, such as emphasis on economic incentives and decentralization, to which Guevara was violently opposed, and that he and Castro came to an abrupt parting of ways over one or more of these issues.

In any event, Castro in the spring and summer of 1965 embarked on economic programs and policies for economic incentives which could not have been pleasing to Guevara and which seemed clearly designed to meet Soviet desires. Castro publicly announced that 1965 was to be a "year of agriculture" and explicitly rejected the idea (originally pushed by Guevara) that Cuba could industrialize in a short period of time. To any observer, it appeared that the Soviets must have laid down the law and stated that the price of economic support was adoption of rational economic practices. In the meantime, Guevara's protégés in the Cuban government lost their positions of influence, and Guevara's ideas became as invisible as Guevara himself. Later, a new identification with Guevara's image became politically desirable to Castro as a result of public speculation over Guevara's fate by Trotskyites and others (but never by pro-Moscow communists).

The Dominican Crisis and the Seeds of Division

Just as the Soviet-Cuban friendship of 1965 was in full flower and the 1964 Havana agreements were demonstrating their viability in the form of new harmony in the Latin American communist movement (and new Chinese frustrations), the picture was suddenly and dramatically changed by the late April Dominican crisis. In the flurry of excitement which followed the U.S. landings and the "constitutionalist" resistance, fuel was added to all the private fires of the movement. The Soviets and their followers in Latin America seized upon the temporary successes of the rebels in resisting "U.S. imperialist intervention" as proof of their long-standing contention that communists in Latin America could best advance their interests by riding on the back of authentic bourgeois-democratic movements. The Chinese and Trotskyites, at the other extreme, pointed an accusing finger at the Soviets and Cubans for confining assistance to the rebels to protests at the U.N., and they insisted that this was proof that revolutionaries could only succeed by rejecting the "revisionist" embrace of both Moscow and Havana. Castro, caught in the middle, had no ready means of disproving either contention and thus began to feel distinctly uneasy about his new closeness to the Soviets. As the summer and fall of 1965 passed, this unease grew until by late in the year Castro must have felt an almost unbearable psychological need to demonstrate his independence from Moscow and regain the respect of the insurrectionist groups in Latin America which had always provided his most ardent support.

A major contribution to this Cuban unease must have been the Soviet attempt after the Dominican crisis to sell the well-worn theme of popular front tactics rather than guerrilla insurgency as the requirement of the moment. If, as seems most likely, the main Soviet interest in the 1964 Havana conference compromise had been the isolation of the Chinese, then by mid-1965 Moscow must already have been looking for ways to back off from the more expensive aspects of the compromise. Soviet tactics had already produced a seemingly self-sustained conflict between Castro and Mao Tse-tung, and elsewhere in the hemisphere pro-Chinese groups were a declining threat to the established parties.

There is every reason to believe that even as the Soviets were making their compromise with the Cubans at the end of 1964, they hoped that this tactical "step forward" would clear the way for two steps backward to a position more suited to Latin American realities. The move toward Castroism at the Havana conference was superficial at best. For all its militant wording, the main stress of the Havana communiqué was on the right of each communist party to determine its own "correct line" and to implement it without competition from externally supported splinter groups. Hence, if a party in one of the six countries of "freedom fighters" later decided that changed circumstances required de-emphasizing violent tactics, Castro was still restrained from supporting other groups by the communiqué's injunction against "all factional activity." The Dominican crisis, in the eyes of Moscow and the traditional parties, signified precisely this sort of "changed circumstances." As one Soviet writer exclaimed in May 1965, "If the Cuban revolution ushered in an age of people's democratic, socialist revolutions in the Western Hemisphere, the present developments in Dominica [sic] are the beginning of a new period, in which the conditions are being created for broad national anti-imperialist fronts to resist North American imperialism."[4] Soviet propaganda insisted that the U.S. was entering a period of "big stick imperialism" which would drive moderate "Boschista" reformers into the arms of the communists, so long as the communists avoided frightening them with overly radical words and deeds.

In the summer and fall of 1965, the international communist apparatus geared up to push this theme on every possible occasion. The Prague-based *World Marxist Review* devoted most of its August issue to Latin American questions, and in each article the same thesis appeared: Armed struggle will come soon enough, the important thing for now is to form broad alliances with all groups opposed to imperialism; to this end, communists should play down partisan slogans and deeds which might repel moderate allies. As a corollary to this thesis, the *World Marxist Review* authors pushed hard on the idea that the key factor in Castro's victory in Cuba had been the "broad united front" which supported him, not the guerrilla tactics which the Cubans subsequently espoused throughout the hemisphere.

Popular Fronts

In addition to the articles on Latin America, the August *World Marxist Review* contained two articles pointing out the continuing relevance of the decisions made by the Seventh Comintern Congress—the congress which had marked the dramatic turn to a popular front line in 1935. The summer and fall of 1965 repeated Soviet use of Seventh Congress themes in theoretical publications as well as in special meetings called to commemorate the thirtieth anniversary of the congress. The resurrection of these themes was by no means tied exclusively to the Latin American situation. Occasional suggestions that these were suited to current communist needs, particularly in Western Europe, had been seen in Soviet publications well before the Dominican crisis. But the U.S. military involvement in the Dominican Republic and the escalation of fighting in Vietnam gave substantial encouragement to Soviet advocates of increased worldwide use of united-front or popular-front tactics. The decisions of the 1935 congress, which condemned "left sectarianism" within the communist movement and authorized alliances with all forces opposed to fascism, were ideally suited to a Russian counteroffensive aimed at isolating both the Chinese "Stalinists" and the U.S. "imperialists."

In October 1965, two separate international conferences were held, one in Prague and one in Moscow, for the ostensible purpose of analyzing the current applicability of the 1935 Comintern decisions.[5] Large foreign communist contingents appeared at both conferences, and the papers and speeches delivered at them were given extensive distribution in international communist media.

Both the extent of Latin American communist participation in the conferences and the references to Latin America in the conference documents make it evident that this continent was among the areas where the Soviets considered the doctrines of 1935 particularly useful. Indeed, in the aftermath of the Dominican crisis, the logic of the Seventh Congress was applicable in a unique sense to Latin America, where the spectre of "U.S. imperialist intervention" could be conjured up as an "external enemy" of both a "socialist fatherland" (in this case Cuba) and the Boschista democratic left. This concept was implicit in much of the Soviet propaganda of the period, which increasingly described the "external enemy" with such epithets as "Nazi-like." It was also made explicit by at least one participant in the Moscow conference. B. T. Rudenko, head of the Latin American Institute of the U.S.S.R. Academy of Sciences, stated in his presentation: ". . . in the period of the 7th Comintern Congress, . . . plans were being hatched by German imperialism. At present, under different conditions but with analogous claims, there is U.S. imperialism."[6]

What was all this activity designed to achieve? Who were the Soviets trying to persuade or to overwhelm with logic? Not the Chinese, certainly, for one of the major purposes of these exercises on the theme of anti-imperialist unity was to demonstrate how intransigent and unreasonable the Maoists were. The obvious targets were the members of the international communist movement who were influenced by "leftist" trends in the movement but were not all the way in the Chinese camp, who were dubious about "peaceful coexistence" and Khrushchev's talk of "peaceful roads to socialism," and who were unmoved by references to post-Stalinist Soviet party congresses. To these targets—among them the Cubans and Venezuelan communists—the Seventh Congress decisions were an ideal pretext for pushing Khrushchevism without Khrushchev and for attacking Mao's "left sectarianism" without naming the Chinese.

V. VENEZUELAN "REVOLUTION," 1965: IDEOLOGICAL BATTLEGROUND

Soviet-PCV Maneuvering

All the ideological maneuvering related to the November 1964 Havana conference and the April–May 1965 Dominican crisis was directly relevant to the Venezuelan communist movement and probably had its most direct repercussions there. Prior to the Havana conference, the Venezuelan communist movement had been afflicted with growing divergencies, many of which derived from the failure of the FALN attempts to disrupt the 1963 elections. In January 1964, the Movement of the Revolutionary Left (MIR), the communists' chief partners in the FALN, split after a public declaration by MIR leader José Vicente Rangel opposing continued use of guerrilla warfare. At the same time, a physical division had developed in the communist party (PCV) as a result of the imprisonment of many of the top PCV leaders. The imprisoned leaders, among them Jesus Faria, Gustavo Machado, and Pompevo Marquez, retained their party titles, but the de facto leadership had passed into the hands of younger militants of more firmly Castroite inclinations.

Although there was no direct evidence that any major faction of the PCV wished to scuttle the armed struggle entirely, as MIR leader Rangel had urged, the divisions within the PCV seemed increasingly to follow lines of ideology. An April 1964 statement by the imprisoned communist leaders focused on unspecified "errors of the recent past which it is henceforth necessary to avoid," while an April 1964 PCV plenum (controlled by middle-level PCV leaders) reasserted forcefully that "the path to victory is that of armed struggle."[1]

The attitude of the Soviets and Chinese toward the PCV during most of 1964 also reflected this ideological cleavage. After the February 1964 conclusion of a *Komosomolskava Pravda* series on the FALN the Soviet press became almost totally silent on the Venezuelan armed struggle, concentrating instead on less militant themes, such as "liberating Venezuelan political prisoners."[2] In late spring, the Soviet news agency TASS ran several items on the Venezuelan people's interest in restoring diplomatic ties with the U.S.S.R., a theme which had been noticeably absent from Soviet propaganda since 1961. Still later, beginning on July 17, *Pravda* began a series of articles based on interviews with the then soft-line MIR leader Américo Chacon.[3] The Chinese, on the other hand, became progressively more ecstatic over FALN guerrilla operations.

Soviet behavior during this period gave no indication that Moscow would decide at the November Havana conference to come out openly in favor of continued armed struggle by the Venezuelan communists. What was visible was the new Soviet willingness to do battle with the Chinese in regard to the specifics of Latin American revolution, which was indicated in the July and August *Kommunist* articles on the Latin American liberation movement. Thus, a few months later, the *World Marxist Review* broke its long silence on the Venezuelan communist movement. The October issue of this journal contained a lengthy article by a Venezuelan communist,

Carlos Lopez, explaining the PCV line decided upon at the April PCV plenum.

The views expressed in the Carlos Lopez article bore the clear earmarks of a compromise between the two PCV factions. On the one hand, it reaffirmed that "the main form of struggle will be that of the classical 'guerrilla' or partisan warfare in the rural localities . . ." On the other, it admitted past mistakes in "attaching too little importance to the socio-economic struggle," and spoke of the need to "combat erroneous concepts with regard to legal mass work." "Clearly any concept that denies the need for work among the masses and sees armed struggle as an absolute should be vigorously rejected," stated Lopez.[4]

The appearance of even this carefully qualified endorsement of the Venezuelan armed struggle was a definite victory for PCV gamesmanship in the Sino-Soviet dispute since the actual prospects for the PCV–FALN armed effort in Venezuela had in no sense improved. In fact the Yugoslavs spoke out openly in October 1964, with the view that the FALN armed struggle was succeeding only in isolating the MIR and the PCV from the Venezuelan people, who were tired of terror.[5]

Part of the Yugoslav concern in this matter may have stemmed from irritation at the way the PCV was courting Peking to extract increased help from Moscow. Starting in early July, a PCV delegation headed by Eduardo Gallegos Mancera began traveling abroad, first to Cuba, then to Communist China, later to North Vietnam, finally to the U.S.S.R. and several of the Eastern European communist capitals. Like salesmen playing on rivalries among neighbors to sell prestige products, the PCV representatives were able to offer each communist power the chance to outdo competitors in support of a "deserving liberation war." Significantly, the last major stop of the PCV delegation was in Moscow, placing the Soviets dramatically on the spot. And sure enough, at the Moscow World Youth Forum in mid-September 1964, Khrushchev publicly embraced the PCV-FALN representatives in the strongest endorsement a Soviet leader had yet given them.[6] Soviet journalists were able to extract some Soviet-line statements out of the Venezuelan delegates during their visit, but it was the PCV which clearly gained from the new Soviet engagement in their area.

After Khrushchev's fall, the Gallegos delegation wound up its Eastern European visits and returned to Moscow in early November, presumably to determine its bargaining position with the new Soviet leadership. By then it may be assumed that the Soviets were already trying to lay the groundwork for the Havana communist conference at the end of the month. Hence they were hardly in a position to cold-shoulder the Venezuelans. Indeed, starting in early November 1964, *Pravda* and *Izvestia* suddenly began carrying short items on "partisan warfare" in Venezuela.

When all the Latin American communist parties gathered in Havana at the month's end, the Soviet-approved recommendations of the meeting called not only for "active support" for the freedom fighters of Venezuela and five other Latin American countries, but it also called upon all signatories "to organize on the scale of the entire continent an active movement of solidarity of all the Latin American peoples with the liberation struggle of Venezuela."[7] On January 14, in a rare front-page editorial in

Pravda entitled "Latin America Struggles," the Soviets again gave explicit approval to the FALN armed struggle: "In Venezuela, Guatemala, and various other countries, patriots with weapons in hand are waging a just struggle in defense of their national interests."

This was to be the high point of Soviet support for the Venezuelan armed struggle. The decline was partially a result of Moscow's previously noted success in sowing serious dissensions between Cuba and Communist China, but another factor seems to have been involved: a growing Soviet recognition that other things might be gained in Latin America if Moscow's ties with terrorist activities such as those in Venezuela could be toned down. It was just at this time that Soviet ties with Chile were being reestablished and Moscow clearly hoped that these ties would give the world an image of the U.S.S.R. as a peace-loving nation. On April 12, 1965, two leading Soviet Latin Americanists S. Mikhailov and A. Shugovsky, were to state in *Pravda*, ". . . the establishment of diplomatic relations between the U.S.S.R. and Chile caused great repercussions throughout Latin America. . . . A number of Latin American countries want to put an end to isolation in foreign policy."

Venezuela was undoubtedly one of the places where the Soviets looked for, and may well have seen, "repercussions" of this sort. Sometime between January and early March, the Soviets sent two experienced correspondents, V. Polyakovsky and V. Kobysh, to Venezuela for a fairly lengthy visit. Their subsequent articles in *Pravda* and *Izvestia* indicate that they saw a great deal of Venezuela and were able to talk to both communist leaders (*Pravda* on March 2 printed a lengthy interview with imprisoned

PCV leader Jesus Faria) and government representatives. Inevitably they got a much different picture of Venezuela than that brought to Moscow by the Gallegos delegation. Not only was Faria a representative of a softer-line group within the PCV, but the personal experiences of the two correspondents must have given them strong reason to doubt that there was any real "revolutionary situation" in Venezuela. Their articles, though not complimentary to the Venezuelan government, provided little fodder for any Soviets who might have favored the harder-line PCV elements.

The Beltramini affair. Whatever the Soviets, or some Soviets, may have been thinking about alternative courses of action in Venezuela, it was soon demonstrated that they were still actively fulfilling their commitments made at the November Havana conference. In the last days of March 1965, the Venezuelan government intercepted two communist couriers bringing some $330,000 into the country. Although no proof of origin or destination of the money was established, it seemed almost certain that it was earmarked for the PCV-FALN and had come via the Italian Communist Party from Moscow or an Eastern European capital. The amount of money was too great to be merely a subsidy of normal party operations; it had to be largely slated for support of the FALN guerrilla operations. One of the couriers, an Italian citizen named Beltramini, had close ties to the Moscow-oriented Italian Communist Party. The Italian party, by virtue of both its location and its political stance in the world communist movement, was not a logical conduit for either Cuban or Chinese funds, but it certainly was for Soviet money.

Whatever the source of Beltramini's funds, there are other convincing indications that Moscow was fulfilling its end of the Havana accords in early 1965. The Venezuelan guerrilla movement did show a new burst of vigor in the early months of the year, while Castro's behavior indicated that he was generally satisfied with Moscow's good faith. After the Beltramini affair, however, the question of Soviet support for the FALN insurgency becomes fuzzier. In the first weeks thereafter, there must have been a period in which the PCV and FALN were short of funds as new courier arrangements were made. One sign that this may have been the case was the disappearance of one of the PCV publications, *El Siglo* in late May, apparently due to financial problems. But in addition, if the Soviets were looking for a pretext for reducing funds for the Venezuelan armed struggle, the Beltramini affair certainly provided one. Moscow could demand better security, claim lack of ready funds, or simply stall by exhibiting bureaucratic lethargy. As 1965 wore on, events both within the Venezuelan communist movement and on the international communist scene suggested that just such a stall might be occurring. In addition to the doctrinal maneuvers over the Dominican crisis and the Seventh Comintern Congress anniversary, there were signs of a parallel stinginess on the part of both the U.S.S.R. and the Venezuelan Communist Party toward the FALN armed struggle.

The democratic peace line. The theoretical line taken by the PCV during 1964—after Leoni's electoral victory and before the Havana communist conference—was never clear-cut. By the communists' own admission, they were undergoing serious internal difficulties and were thinking in short-range terms. Although the party remained committed to armed struggle, it was unable to produce a forceful reply to MIR soft-liner Rangel's declaration at the beginning of the year repudiating guerrilla tactics. Many of the party leaders apparently kept hoping for a dramatic turn of events, such as a military coup, which would reunite the Venezuelan left and vindicate their extremist line. Guerrilla activities proceeded haltingly as the PCV sought to "sharpen contradictions" in the Venezuelan government and "expose the true nature" of Leoni.

When a compromise was more-or-less reached in the fall of 1964, in the form of the Gomez article in the *World Marxist Review*, the PCV line remained defensive and equivocal. The party clearly wished to emphasize an expansion of legal, non-armed activities, but it offered no new rationale for a change in tactics. Armed struggle as a means of bringing on a crisis and a truly "revolutionary situation" remained the dominant theme of PCV theorizing, although now there was an additional tactical gambit: The FALN declared itself willing to end armed operations if the government met a series of demands—amnesty of political prisoners, legality of the PCV and MIR, reinstatement of pro-FALN officers into the national army, guarantees of constitutional liberties, and a "'national economic policy."[8]

It was in this period from 1964 to early 1965, that the seeds of the subsequent open split of the PCV-FALN took root and began to grow. Statements at the end of 1966 by Douglas Bravo and other leaders of the breakaway FALN group refer back to the PCV policy in 1964 with contempt, decrying the vacillations of the party leadership and its repeated fruitless political maneuvering. All of this, in their view, seriously delayed the development of a unified politico-military leadership of the FALN and repeatedly stymied the development of momentum in the rural guerrilla war. Some of them apparently said so at the time, judging from the defensiveness of PCV on this question in early 1965. At the seventh PCV plenum in April 1965, the PCV declared repeatedly that the "truce periods" of April and December 1964 had been "politically and militarily correct," whereas "the real utilization of the truce periods to improve the armed detachments organically and militarily was insufficient."[9]

Toward the end of 1965 there was also a sharp disagreement between Bravo's faction and other party leaders over whether the main danger to the movement lay in deviation to the left or to the right. According to Bravo, in a late 1966 interview, "When some political leaders insisted that the chief danger —and they began to say so in 1964—came from the left, we refuted them by saying that this was false because in Venezuela the proper conditions for such a development did not exist."[10]

What became of this debate between the Havana conference of November 1964 and the seventh PCV plenum the following April, neither side has been willing to disclose. Bravo hints in this same interview that there was in fact a brief rapprochement: "At the beginning of the year 1965, the revolutionary movement was provided with a guideline in regard to the problem of armed struggle which without a doubt came closer to what was proper and viable. . . ." Presumably what Bravo was referring to was the FALN "military plan for 1965," which, as quoted from Cuban sources by the Venezuelan press, called mainly for improved coordination of the various rural and urban activities of the FALN and increased involvement of the peasantry in FALN activities.[11]

The April 1965 plenum. These early dissensions and intra-party bickering were slight when compared to the repercussions of the April 1965 PCV plenum, which laid down the line of democratic peace. On the surface, the documents of this plenum appeared to represent a compromise in the spirit of the November 1964 Havana accords. They spoke of the "consolidation, amplification, and escalation of the guerrilla movement" and of the "reconstruction of a single politico-military leadership" from top to bottom of the FLN-FALN.[12] All of this sounded like a sincere and long-term commitment to a rural-based guerrilla war and appeared consistent with the FALN "military plan for 1965" publicized by Cuba. But in addition to this, under the heading of the program for a democratic peace, the party had outlined a policy of alliances so broad as to be unthinkable without a corresponding cutback in partisan warfare. It was this feature of the April plenum decisions which raised eyebrows among interested observers of Venezuelan communist politics, and it was this same feature which surely gave Castro pause for reflection on the compromise he had agreed to in November of 1964.

Castro's later comments of the democratic peace formula are so revealing of his state of mind in the period after the Havana conference that they are worth quoting at some length:

The leadership of the Venezuelan Communist Party began by talking about democratic peace. Many people wondered what was meant by democratic peace. We did not understand, but still we wanted to understand. We asked several Venezuelan leaders what was meant. Then we learned about the well-known and formulated theory of those tactics and that maneuver which was not that of abandoning the war. No. It concerned a maneuver to broaden the base, to destroy the government, to weaken it and undermine it.

We could not understand it at all. However, we had faith, and we waited . . . although we thought the talk about democratic peace was absurd and ridiculous. . . . At bottom, behind those explanations, lay deceit. They did not say that democratic peace was a maneuver, but that the struggle, that guerrilla warfare, would be stepped up. However this was a lie. At the bottom the intention was to abandon the armed struggle, and the way was just being prepared.[13]

Was the democratic peace formula a deceitful maneuver to prepare the way for abandonment of the armed struggle, as Castro now alleges? The answer almost certainly is yes, and it is also virtually certain that the main target of this deception (or attempted persuasion, depending on one's viewpoint) was Castro and his ideological followers in Venezuela. Whether the formula was urged on the PCV by Moscow or developed independently by pro-Moscow Venezuelan communists is uncertain and not vitally important. The key fact was that the formula fitted perfectly into the carefully modulated debates Moscow was then organizing around the popular front theme of the Seventh Comintern Congress. Surely it was a reference to this classic popular front doctrine that Castro was talking about when he stated in the above quotation: "We asked several Venezuelan leaders what was meant. Then we learned about the well-known and formulated theory of those tactics. . . ."

Democratic peace, as formulated in the docu-

ments of the seventh PCV plenum, did in fact con-
form almost exactly to the classical popular front
doctrine. Specifically, the PCV proposal called upon
all Venezuelan communists to support an "alternative government" to that of Leoni. This alternative
government was clearly not to be a revolutionary or
even necessarily a procommunist one, but was to
"include all those opposed to the Betancourt policy
and who are in favor of those changes indicated by
the democratic peace [program]." Indeed, it was to
include "in the front lines those sectors and person-
alities who within the same [Leoni] government are
opposed to this [Betancourtist] policy." In other
words, this alternative government of democratic
peace was to be a government in the traditional
mode of Venezuelan politics, merely one which
would give the communists more freedom and more
opportunities for expanding their influence. Indeed,
the seventh plenum resolutions specifically allowed
for the possibility that the proposed democratic
peace government might start working against the
communists: "If it [the new government] develops
in the opposite and disorderly direction due to imperialism, betraying the program of democratic
peace, we will fight it."

The program assigned to the "government of
democratic peace" also involved a definite toning-
down of the past PCV position. Its demands were
close to those proclaimed the previous fall as the
price of peace, but it was less specific. The "min-
imum program of democratic peace" consisted of
"general amnesty, legality of the PCV and MIR,
full implementation of the constitution, freedom of
the press, economic measures for the people and
against hunger, and a foreign policy of friendship

with all the people of the world." Gone was the specific demand for "reinstatement of democratic-minded army officers" into the national armed forces, as well as all specific demands in the economic and foreign policy fields.

Finally, the seventh plenum resolutions, while speaking of expanded rural guerrilla activities, also asserted that "during the present phase, the armed activities in the cities cannot predominate," and must be restricted to those actions "which will not raise unnecessary obstacles to the development of non-armed mass struggle. . . ." And a hint of the internal struggles to come was contained in the final admonition of the resolutions, which stated, "It is really indispensable to unleash forcefully a serious ideological battle, which brings to the minds of our comrades the greatest possible clarity regarding the importance and the role played today by the renewal of this work among the masses."[14]

Selling the Great Retreat

It would appear, both from Castro's comments about meetings with PCV leaders and from the apparent lack of movement within the PCV during the summer of 1965, that for several months after the April PCV plenum the party leaders were quietly trying to sell the new democratic peace line to the Cubans and the Venezuelan Castroites. The PCV leaders may also have been waiting to see what results the Soviets would have in their international campaign to propagandize popular front theories. Additionally, they may have been waiting for a particularly dramatic failure in the FALN military campaign to provide the right atmosphere for pushing their revisionist thesis.

At any rate, there was no obvious PCV retreat from armed struggle between April and September 1965. Rural military operations by the FALN continued sporadically and received the normal small coverage in Soviet media. In late summer, another PCV-FALN delegation headed by Eduardo Gallegos was travelling in communist countries, first at the Romanian party congress in late July and then at an August exhibition in Prague on the Venezuelan armed struggle. Interestingly, no one from the left wing of the international communist movement has accused Moscow or the PCV of failing to *support* FALN armed actions in this period. Castro merely charged that PCV leaders were secretly *planning* to liquidate the armed struggle. Douglas Bravo has not gone even that far, perhaps because he had agreed to the democratic peace line (all his writings indicate he has fewer ideological differences with orthodox communism than Castro), or because he has wished to avoid offending anyone within the PCV whom he might be able to win over to his side in the Venezuelan communist factional struggle.

Moscow, while still seeming to carry out its part of the Havana 1964 accords concerning support of Venezuelan "freedom fighters," was also doing everything it could to sell Castro on the popular front line. In addition to the international orchestration of popular front themes, there was apparently a Soviet attempt to continue the Togliatti stratagem of arranging regional bilateral and multilateral communist meetings. The Chilean Communist Party, the most influential non-ruling communist party in the hemisphere, was given a key role in this effort. In

June, a Chilean CP delegation en route to Moscow spent two or three days in Cuba conferring with Castro. Then in October the Chilean CP, which had taken an even more moderate, popular-front stance following the talks in Moscow, held its thirteenth party congress with guest delegations from over thirty other communist parties.

The Chilean party congress, which took place October 10–17, clearly had significance beyond the Chilean domestic scene. The Soviets honored it with the highest-ranking communist official they had ever sent to a Latin American communist party congress, Presidium member A. P. Kirilenko. There has been no indication as to what went on at the various closed meetings at the congress, but the Soviets clearly saw these as a vital opportunity to dramatize their endorsement of the Chilean communist approach and point out its relevance to other parties of the hemisphere. Most of the Latin American communist parties were represented there, and it would have been difficult for any to miss the point. For the benefit of those who were missing the conferences in Moscow and Prague on the Seventh Comintern Congress anniversary there was a lengthy speech in Santiago by the Bulgarian delegate glorifying the popular front era and the continuing applicability of these doctrines today.[15]

If the Soviets thought the Cubans would be convinced by the Chilean communist example or words, they were victims of overconfidence. The communiqué of the June meeting between Castro and the Chilean communists was at best cool and correct.[16] The speech of the Cuban delegate at the Chilean party congress, Lionel Soto, only barely skirted a repudiation of the popular front theme.[17] Finally, there can be no doubt that by mid-October the Cubans were already gravely concerned by events in the Venezuelan communist movement, which could no longer be disguised as anything but a rejection of Castroism. The Venezuelans, interestingly, were among the few Latin American communist parties not listed as attending the Chilean meeting.[18]

The Open Break with Armed Struggle

The open break by the PCV soft-line leadership had come about a month earlier. The intra-party offensive became public knowledge in early September with a series of articles in the weekly communist newspaper, ¿Qué?, forcefully restating the democratic peace thesis and defending it against criticism from other factions of the Venezuelan far left. Before the appearance of these articles, there had been occasional rumblings of differences within the FLN over the doctrine the PCV Politburo was trying to sell. In August, for example, the Caracas press had published a June 1965 letter by PCV politburo member Pompeyo Marquez in which he told other party leaders that MIR members of the FLN had serious difficulty in accepting the democratic peace line. Not only did they consider it "timid and even conciliatory," but they objected to the unilateral way the slogan had been launched—without consulting other members of the FLN.[19] But prior to September the opposing sides had refrained from stating their differences openly.

The ostensible reason given by the PCV leadership for the open break in September was that the MIR had been making "impudent" and "infamous"

55

charges against the PCV, accusing it of following an "opportunist" policy, of proposing "rightist tactics," involving "conciliations" before imperialism, and of deceiving the revolutionary forces and leading them to a defeat.[20] The PCV insisted that such scurrilous attacks required a forceful reply to set the record straight.

Later statements by the dissident Bravo faction of the FALN, however, give a more persuasive explanation of the timing. According to Bravo, it was the repeated Venezuelan government successes against the guerrillas in the fall of 1965 which opened the way for the PCV doctrine of retreat. The defeats suffered by the guerrillas in late 1965, stated Bravo, "produced disappointment, discouragement, and skepticism among certain segments within the revolutionary movement," and in this atmosphere the idea of retreat was able to take root.[21]

Documents of the PCV itself also confirm that the guerrilla defeats in the fall of 1965 were a major factor in the decision to launch the internal political offensive at that time. The September 1965 PCV "reply" to the MIR implied clearly that the tactics of survival, if nothing else, required a pulling-back in the guerrilla effort:

There is no need to be very intelligent to understand that we have to tackle the tasks of national liberation by stages and that we have to know how to fight well and to avoid fighting in unfavorable terrain and committing too many errors. . . .

This tactical line [of democratic peace], which takes into account the insoluble difficulties of the ruling groups, also takes into consideration the temporary difficulties of the liberation movement. . . .[22]

Two internal PCV documents which Castro made public in his speech of March 13, 1967 serve to clarify the PCV strategy of the period still further. The first, a letter signed on November 7, 1965 by PCV politburo members Pompeyo Marquez, Teodoro Petkoff, and Freddy Munoz, stated that because of "continuous blows and setbacks," the movement was "not at present in a condition to continue an open, frontal clash with its enemies . . . as a result the party must fall back on the military front and recommend suspension of armed action in order to regroup its forces and prepare them for a new revolutionary stage."[23] The second document, a letter of the same date signed by other PCV leaders, reveals that for some audiences the defensive explanation given above was to be deemphasized in favor of a rationale stressing the gains to be achieved through mass action and broad unity of leftist forces. Both letters were sent with an introductory note explaining the differences in approach:

As you can see, the remarks and conclusions are the same: the falling back of the guerrillas and the UTC [urban combat units] and a change of tactics to emphasize political initiative. . . . Yet there is a shade of difference. Our document places political motivation first, and then the motivation of blows received. For the other comrades, that order is reversed. The blows received are a very important factor, but we must not give the explanation that it is fundamentally because of this factor that we are going to introduce changes in our tactics. . . . As a matter of fact, we should have fallen back even before sustaining the setbacks.

The final suggestion made in the covering note just quoted, with its hint of petulance at the diehards who had frustrated any earlier implementation of the democratic peace line, merely dramatizes the de facto importance of the guerrilla defeats in PCV efforts to shift directions.

Democratic peace unveiled. The September 1965 reiteration of the democratic peace doctrine, which the PCV leaders claimed was a reply to MIR slanders, went well beyond the requirements of a reply. It was a forceful statement of the popular front thesis which hinted strongly at corollaries of democratic peace which had carefully been left unstated in the April plenum resolutions. Chief among these corollaries was, of course, the fallback in guerrilla warfare, and the PCV tactics included an obvious effort to discredit those who were still pressing for continued FALN military action. The September declaration of the PCV stated that the party would henceforth seek to "avoid an unnecessary defeat of the revolutionary movement brought about by sectarianism, arrogance, and [the] impatient small bourgeoisie."[24]

In the internal PCV documents made public by Castro, the PCV leaders were even more forthright, both on the ramifications of the democratic peace doctrine and the wickedness of its detractors. The full PCV argument went as follows:

Political initiatives:

The processes under way enable the revolutionary movement to take the initiative on the political front. However it will be necessary for the FALN to order the guerrillas and the UTC to fall back. It is not a new truce but something more profound; it is the start of a new tactical phase in which, instead of combining every form of struggle, action by the guerrillas and the UTC will be suspended, and first place will be given to political initiatives, the grouping of the left, the promotion of new forces the struggle against Betancourtism; unity, organization, and mobilization of the masses; alliance with the nationalistic sectors of the armed forces, action by labor in support of its demands, the battle against repression, and so forth.

Negative results of armed actions:

Weak armed operations that merely repeat similar preceding operations, without making truly meaningful progress, are: 1) hampering political action and the regrouping of forces against the Betancourtist gorillas*; 2) letting the Betancourtist gorilla clique retain its alliances; 3) acting as a broke, preventing an acceleration of the disintegration of the "broad base"; and 4) destroying conviction and faith in the correct general strategy of the revolutionary movement, whose foundation was laid by the Third Congress of the PCV and later added to by successive plenary meetings of the party.

It is especially necessary to watch the uncontrollable, the bad ones . . . the rebels, and also to actively defend the policy, tactics, and leadership of the Communist youth and the Communist party from the attacks of the MIRist anarchic-adventurist group.[25]

FALN versus PCV

It is apparent from the tone of these documents that during most of 1965 the PCV considered the FALN to be a tool of the party, the "military arm" of the PCV. The PCV could decide in a closed plenum to change the FALN line and the line would change, albeit with a certain amount of grumbling from unconsulted MIR members. Likewise, the PCV leadership could call for temporary truces or halts in FALN armed actions, as they had done repeatedly since 1963, and the guerrillas by and large would follow instructions. This was as it should be according to traditional communist patterns. Front organizations (as distinguished from popular fronts, which are

* A term Latin American leftists apply to rightist enemies.

broad coalitions, not necessarily dominated by communists), such as the FLN and FALN, have been created by the hundreds by communist parties over the years, all with certain basic similarities: popular figureheads, broad membership, and vague goals to give the front maximum public acceptability, combined with covert communist control. The ultimate party control has customarily been assured by the strategic placement of party members at strategic points in the front and by the party's monopoly on outside financial assistance.

Up until late 1965, the FALN had conformed moderately well to the traditional model, a fact which has been acknowledged by those most disgruntled at the way the PCV was running the FALN. "The revolutionary leadership of the party," said Castro in his March 13, 1967 speech, "in an effort to direct the guerrilla forces from the plains and from the capital, did not do what was necessary. . . ." In the PCV view, said Castro, "the guerrillas were really not considered a force capable of growing and of seizing revolutionary power in countries such as ours. Instead they were considered an instrument of agitation, a political instrument, a tool for negotiations. . . . " Fabricio Ojeda, a member of the dissident Bravo group, wrote a letter to Castro in June 1966 which explained the PCV's financial control over the FALN : ". . . our financial problem . . . stems from the fact that the Political Bureau has been in control of this department. Hitherto, all assistance given the revolutionary movement has been concentrated in this organization and used as a function of its policy. That is, it financially throttled the guerrilla centers."[26]

Finances. The Beltramini affair and the November

1964 conference results had strongly suggested that, in the period prior to the PCV "retreat," someone other than Castro (presumable the U.S.S.R.) was supplying the bulk of the funds for the FALN warfare. Ojeda's comments, and the fact that he sent them to Castro, confirm this fact, and a rather interesting picture is completed. In late 1964, the U.S.S.R. asserts full responsibility for aiding the Venezuelan "liberation war" by sending one, and perhaps several, shipments of money on the scale of several hundred thousand dollars. Then, in late 1965, the funds abruptly dry up, precisely at a time when the PCV takes the bull by the horns and declares that a fallback in the guerrilla struggle is necessary. It is hard to escape the conclusion that following Khrushchev's fall the Soviets had been consciously seeking control of the reins in Venezuela's guerrilla movement in order to draw them up short.

The mechanics of the Soviet-PCV-FALN financial relationship are difficult to calculate. There is reason to believe that as of about October 1965 no one in the Venezuelan revolutionary movement was getting much money from abroad. *New York Times* correspondent H. J. Maidenberg reported from Caracas on October 13 that there was a growing optimism among Venezuelan security officials because "arms and financial aid from Havana, Moscow and Peking has [sic] practically dried up this year."[27] There seem to be two plausible explanations for the cutoff of Soviet funds. The first possibility is that Moscow delivered an ultimatum to the PCV that no more funds would be forthcoming until the PCV brought a halt to this counterproductive guerrilla business. Such an ultimatum could have been effective because the PCV, like the Cubans, had almost completely lost its option of turning towards Peking by agreeing to the 1964 Havana accords. The second explanation is that the PCV leaders realized that the only way the democratic peace line would prevail would be if the FALN guerrillas were starved into submission. Then the PCV leaders might have requested that Moscow withhold funds to allow the PCV to display its empty coffers. These explanations are not mutually exclusive, of course. If there was a Soviet ultimatum, there were undoubtedly a number of PCV soft-liners who welcomed it; likewise, if PCV leaders themselves asked for a cutback, they may well have asked for it in the form of an ultimatum in order to give them maximum leverage against the hard-liners.

The FALN on its own. Whether the Soviets and PCV soft-liners actually thought they could bring the FALN guerrillas to heel at this point is not at all certain. In the past, truces had been carried out on party instructions, but always with the promise of more funds for fighting later. Now the party was asking for a truce without that promise. Furthermore, the truce that was being requested was of a duration which would require the guerrillas virtually to abandon a whole way of life and to allow prided skills to atrophy. Both the Soviets and the PCV soft-liners may well have underestimated these factors, but they must have at least recognized them. They probably judged that despite the obstacles to complete success, they had no alternative but to make an attempt. They may have hoped that the mere fact of having made the attempt would put the PCV in a much better bargaining position with other political forces in Venezuela. In addition, if real gains could be shown on the political front, the pressure on the remaining guerrillas would increase.

Whatever the calculations of the pro-Soviet elements, the timing of the PCV retreat almost guaranteed, unwittingly, the survival of the dissident faction of the FALN. Just at the time that the PCV was drawing its financial props out from under the FALN, the FALN itself, as a separate entity, was gaining significant international stature in the third-world "peoples solidarity" movement which was preparing for the Havana Tricontinent Conference. It was the FALN, not the PCV, which represented the Venezuelan "liberation movement" at the Fourth Afro-Asian Peoples Solidarity Conference in Ghana in May 1965. And it was the FLN (of which FALN is a part) which participated in preparatory meetings for the Tricontinent Conference, which was to meet in January 1966. This fact was of little significance as long as the FLN and FALN were reasonably reliable fronts of the PCV, but it acquired great significance once the PCV Politburo began trying to enforce a cutback in the armed movement in Venezuela.

Every success of past PCV efforts to make the FLN-FALN seem less of a tool of the PCV could now be played back against the soft-line PCV leaders. As long as the PCV could not withdraw from the FALN or purge it of dissidents—and either action would have left the PCV more isolated than before —the FALN and FLN structure could remain a haven for revolutionaries who refused to accept PCV discipline. If internal discipline in the PCV had been complete, continued control over the FALN might have been possible. But discipline was far from complete, and those party leaders who were least inclined to go along with the soft-line majority of the PCV were precisely those who were the PCV representatives in the FLN-FALN. The most prominent among these was Douglas Bravo, who was both a member of the PCV Politburo and commander of the "José Leonardo Chirinos" front of the FALN.

As the division in the Venezuelan communist movement deepened in October and November of 1965, Douglas Bravo became the central figure in the efforts to unify all those opposed to the democratic peace line, and the FLN-FALN framework provided the organizational structure for the dissident movement. The soft-line faction of the PCV, which was in the majority, still retained control of a portion of the FALN, a portion which the PCV naturally claimed was the true FALN, but the larger part of the existing organization apparently leaned towards Bravo. Equally important, where the FALN and not the PCV was represented abroad, the inclination of the FALN representatives was often toward Bravo.

The key step in the unification around Bravo was the establishment of the long-discussed "single political-military leadership of the FALN" on December 10, 1965.[28] This initially involved little more than an agreement "to make use of the existing nucleus of [FALN] leadership" and to reorganize it from top to bottom to make it responsive to this nucleus.[29] None of this was actually accomplished for some months, except on paper, but the intent was clear. Bravo and his supporters (the most prominent being Fabricio Ojeda) intended to end the FALN's status as a communist front, not to make it any less communist, but to make it a Castro-style communist movement in its own right, absorbing as many militant

64

cadres from the PCV and other extreme leftist parties as it could.

The Cuban question mark. Whether the Cubans actively encouraged the dissident movement of Bravo and Ojeda at this point remains open to conjecture. They were, of course, specifically enjoined from doing so by the 1964 Havana conference. But from September 1965 onward, there were repeated signs that Castro was undergoing a strong psychological reaction against past agreements with the Soviets. Indeed, a very strong case can be made for the thesis that Castro's pride had suffered so much under the effects of his apparent sellout to Moscow after Khrushchev's fall that he was looking for every conceivable opportunity to flout Moscow's will, while conforming to the letter of his agreements with the Soviets.

The details of the Soviet-Cuban agreements to which Castro was reacting can for the most part only be surmised, but Castro's earlier behavior in 1965 and the logic of Soviet interests in Cuba point convincingly to certain general outlines of presumed bargains. Aside from the agreements of the 1964 Havana conference, there are three things that the Soviets logically would have tried to commit Castro to in return for continued massive assistance: (1) rationalization of the Cuban economy to minimize waste of Soviet aid; 2) strengthening of the Cuban party to make survival of Cuban communism less dependent on Castro's longevity; and 3) an attitude of Cuban peaceful coexistence toward the U.S. to minimize the U.S. threat to Soviet investments in Cuba.

During most of 1965 there had been signs of willing Cuban compliance with all three of these presumed Soviet demands. The most dramatic Cuban moves had been in the economy, with the eclipse of Che Guevara, long-time advocate of industrialization and moral incentives in labor. Early in 1965, Castro had announced a long-term commitment to development of agriculture in Cuba and had announced introduction of many material incentives in Cuban labor. Elsewhere Cuban compliance was less dramatic, but the Cubans did bow toward peaceful coexistence by remaining quiet about U.S. overflights and Guantanamo, and they did make renewed efforts at developing the Cuban party along more orthodox communist lines.

Suddenly in September and October, Castro made dramatic, flamboyant announcements on three subjects: Che Guevara, the Cuban Party, and relations with the U.S. Che Guevara, an "unperson" since April, was suddenly resurrected, in spirit if not yet in person, in the form of a flattering letter to Castro, and Castro asserted that the debate over moral versus material incentives was still open. In regard to the party, Castro suddenly announced that henceforth the former "United Party of the Socialist Revolution" was to be called the Cuban Communist Party.[30] But beneath this facade of communist orthodoxy was the fact that virtually all of the old-line communists whose party memberships dated from prerevolutionary days had been excluded from positions of influence in the organs of the new party.

Finally, in regard to the U.S., Castro made an unexpected gesture which the Soviets could certainly interpret as "conciliatory" towards the U.S.: He announced that Cubans wishing to leave for the U.S. were free to go if the U.S. would airlift them.[31] Of all of the dramatic gestures, the airlift proposal was

obviously the least thought out; Castro was immediately embarrassed by the vast numbers who wished
to leave his 'socialist paradise' and had to backtrack.
It was almost as if Castro in a fit of irritation had
told the Soviet Ambassador: "All right, you want me
to make a gesture to those Yanqui's; I'll make one
. . . you'll see," and had then searched his mind for
the deed which would most dramatically demonstrate that he was not a Walter Ulbricht, forced to
build a Berlin Wall to keep his people from fleeing.
All of these deeds conformed to the letter of Castro's
presumed agreements with Moscow. But all were
also as far removed from the spirit of those agreements as Castro's imagination could take them.

Thus to return to Castro's other agreement—that
of the 1964 Havana conference—there is every reason to believe that by the time of the PCV Politburo's
retreat from armed struggle in Venezuela, Castro was
prepared to do everything short of open alignment
against the PCV to support the dissident faction of
Bravo and Ojeda. Since there was still no public
split between the PCV and the FLN-FALN, he
could give great encouragement and at least verbal
support to the Castroite dissidents within the FALN
and still justify it as support of a PCV-approved
front, thus steering clear of the Havana conference
injunction against "all factional activity." How much
encouragement and support he was able to give the
Bravo-Ojeda group from October to December 1965
is uncertain, but by the time of the Havana Tricontinent Conference in January 1966, he had developed his techniques for eclipsing the PCV into a fine
art.

THE TRICONTINENT CONFERENCE:
CASTRO UNCHAINED

The January 3–15, 1966 Tricontinent Conference
came at a critical moment in the Soviet-Cuban relationship. Not only did it come at a time when
Castro was feeling a strong psychological need to
demonstrate his independence of mind, but it came
at a moment when one of his major concessions to
Moscow—the 1964 Havana agreement—was being
put to the test by the Venezuelan Communist Party.
If this were not enough, the Tricontinent Conference
itself was being planned by its chief financial backer,
the U.S.S.R., as a grand maneuver for using Castro
against the communist Chinese in the arena of third-
world radicalism. Thus, it would be no exaggeration
to state that the twelve days of the Tricontinent Conference had more impact on Soviet-Cuban relations
than all of the previous thirteen months since the
1964 Havana communist party conference.

Background of the Tricontinent: AAPSO

In its genesis, the Tricontinent Conference was almost entirely unrelated to the 1964 Havana conference. The 1964 conference had been a meeting
of traditional communist party representatives: the
Tricontinent was a much more amorphous assem-
blage of "popular organizations." The 1964 meeting
had been sponsored (if not inspired) by Latin
Americans; the Tricontinent was sponsored (though
also not entirely inspired) by the Afro-Asian Peoples

Solidarity Organization (AAPSO), with permanent headquarters in Cairo. There was a thread of connection between the two meetings, however, because it was the 1964 Havana conference which finally overcame certain political obstacles which had previously prevented AAPSO from expanding its horizons to include Latin America.

AAPSO came into existence at a time when the emerging continent of Africa was looming particularly large in the Soviet view of world opportunities.* The Bandung Conference of Afro-Asian leaders in 1955 had captured the imagination of many Africans, and it had aroused Moscow's interest as having the potential for a movement which could be of critical importance to the U.S.S.R. If the Soviets did not become part of the movement, they would run the risk of being lumped in with the other developed countries which were targets of the movement's anti-Western mood, and, in effect, they would concede to Peking the role of communist representative in the third world. If, on the other hand, they could trade on their eastern extension into Asia to become members of the movement, they stood in a position to use it as an access to African minds. They also could more easily stave off development of the potential antiwhite racism in the movement, which threatened Moscow's influence as much as it did the West's.

Fortunately for the Soviets, the U.A.R.'s President Nasser was also interested in expanding influence in Africa, and the two powers were able to come to terms on a meeting and an organization. The meeting was the nongovernmental First Afro-Asian Peoples

* AAPSO began as AAPSC, the Afro-Asian Peoples Solidarity Committee, but changed its name in 1960.

Solidarity Conference in Cairo, December 1957 to January 1958. The organization was AAPSO, with the Soviets, Egyptians, and Chinese forming a sort of triumvirate of power (and financial support) within the ruling bodies.

By 1964, however, the Sino-Soviet dispute had so rent the organization that its usefulness as an avenue of influence for any of its sponsors had declined drastically. Most of the more moderate and politically significant Afro-Asian groups had left in the face of the incessant bickering of the communist giants, and those that remained were merely out for whatever publicity and financial aid they could get. Moscow and Peking, for their part, were engaged in a bitter struggle for position in the movement. At stake was not simply the limited political benefits which a properly behaved AAPSO could give to the victor; the U.S.S.R.'s very status as an Afro-Asian power was at issue. Both Moscow and Peking realized that the status of the U.S.S.R. in AAPSO might turn out to be a crucial precedent in future Afro-Asian activities such as the proposed "Second Bandung."

It is in this context that the question of Latin American participation in AAPSO (and ultimately the Tricontinent Conference) becomes significant. As early as 1961 the question of involving Latin Americans in AAPSO activities had been raised, and the matter had been shelved for the obvious reasons.[1] Since then, despite repeated discussions of the matter, it had never gotten off that shelf. No formula could be found for selecting Latin American delegations which would satisfy both Moscow and Peking, and neither communist power saw enough to gain from a combined AAPSO-Latin American meeting to make it worth a battle. Moscow already had communist parties amenable to its influence in every Latin American country and hence had little need for further access at the "popular" level. Peking stood to gain only if the majority of Latin American delegations could be of Maoist or at least Castroite stripe. This was at best an unlikely event.

The Winneba AAPSO meeting. The November 1964 Havana conference suddenly altered the AAPSO political equation. The Cubans and the Chinese were now at odds, and Castro was committed to dealing through the established Latin American communist parties. The problem of selecting Latin American delegations thus had an obvious solution: to defer it entirely to the Maximum Leader of Cuba. If Peking wished to protest the makeup of the Latin American contingent, it would be facing a fire-eating third-world revolutionary rather than a stiff Soviet bureaucrat. Moscow could feel quite confident that the Chinese would have to back down before a Cuban-proposed slate of pro-Moscow Latin Americans, with the result that the westward expansion of AAPSO would almost double the forces opposed to Peking in the organization.

A second factor had also entered the picture to make Moscow strongly interested in expanding AAPSO; this was the matter of the next (fifth) Afro-Asian Peoples Solidarity Conference. During AAPSO meetings in 1964, the Chinese had managed to obtain an official endorsement of Peking as the site of the fifth conference. Moscow, however, was determined that the Chinese should be deprived of this honor and this chance to reassert their claims to leadership of Afro-Asia. The obvious way of going about this was to get a majority of AAPSO members to vote for a change in venue, but this threatened to force many Asian AAPSO members who had been showing independence from Peking to rally around the Chinese. The tricontinent idea, on the other hand, offered a very attractive alternative to Moscow. If AAPSO could be submerged in a larger tricontinent movement, the Peking AAPSO conference would be automatically canceled, and the new organization would be under no obligation to meet in the Chinese capital.

These were the factors which were uppermost in Soviet and Chinese minds when the fourth AAPSO conference convened in Winneba, Ghana, May 9–16, 1965. Everything went approximately as expected. The proposal for accepting Cuba's invitation to a Tricontinent Conference in January 1966 was advanced by the Ghanaians. Enthusiastic backing was provided by the Soviets, who also urged that the Havana meeting be considered a regular AAPSO function (hence authorized to decide the question of expanding AAPSO). The Chinese responded icily, pointing out AAPSO's previous commitment to a Peking conference and insisting that the Havana meeting could not be a regular AAPSO meeting.[2]

The results were only a partial Soviet victory. The Tricontinent Conference was formally endorsed, but the Chinese succeeded in gaining reendorsement of their Peking AAPSO conference and in preventing designation of the Tricontinent Conference as a regular AAPSO conference. Peking still recognized the Tricontinent Conference as a serious threat, however; Chinese propaganda media made no reference to it whatsoever between the Winneba meeting and the opening of the conference. The Soviets, on the other hand, evidently felt confident that their partial failures at Winneba could be rectified in Havana. All the AAPSO members were to be present at the Tricontinent Conference, after all, and it did not seem unreasonable to hope that an "official" AAPSO meeting could be convoked on the spot to declare a merger with a tricontinent organization. In any case, Soviet media expressed unqualified enthusiasm over the forthcoming conference, leaving little doubt that Moscow expected to see a tricontinent movement born and AAPSO finally buried at Havana.[3]

The Tricontinent Preparatory Meetings

The mechanism set up at Winneba to prepare for the Tricontinent Conference consisted of an eighteen member preparatory committee (six from each continent) chaired by the Moroccan Mehdi Ben Barka. The six Latin American "popular organizations" on the committee were the Cuban PCC (Communist Party of Cuba), the Venezuelan FLN, the Chilean FRAP (Popular Action Front), the Guatemalan FAR (Rebel Armed Forces), the Uruguayan FIDEL (Left Liberation Front), and the Mexican MLN (National Liberation Movement). All of these except the Mexican MLN met in Cairo September 1–2, 1965 with the delegations from the other continents in the first preparatory meeting for the Tricontinent.

If the Winneba meeting had hinted at Soviet-Cuba collusion against the Chinese, the Cairo meeting seemed to confirm it. At first glance, to be sure, the Latin American members of the preparatory committee did not all appear to be in the Soviet camp, but this was in part because the membership of the

committee had not really been selected at Winneba
—it had been based on earlier formulas for a tricontinent conference which had been proposed by
the Cubans before their 1965 rapprochement with
the Soviets. However, the two members of Castro's
pre-1965 slate which had been most clearly opposed
to Moscow and to the traditional communist parties
were absent at the Cairo meeting. One, the Mexican
MLN, simply did not show up; the other, the Guatemalan Thirteenth of November Revolutionary
Movement, had been replaced at Castro's request
by the communist party-approved FAR.

The Cuban behavior at the Cairo meeting also conformed to the agreements of the 1964 Havana conference. When they were asked for their list of proposed invitations, the Cubans apparently suggested a
list composed exclusively of the traditional Latin
American communist parties or their front groups.
When the Chinese challenged this with a list of their
own followers in the hemisphere, the Cubans and
Soviets compromised on a formula calling for solidarity committees representing all leftist, anti-
imperialist, and liberation groups in each country.
But the final decision on representation was still
to be left entirely in the hands of the Latin American members of the preparatory committee.[4] Thus,
the Soviets could still be reasonably confident that
the Latin American contingent at Havana would be
dominated by the pro-Moscow communist parties.

Divergent Soviet-Cuban Designs

The apparent Soviet optimism over the preparations for the Tricontinent Conference failed to take
into account the evolution in Castro's frame of mind

which was taking place toward the end of 1965. As we have already seen in regard to Che Guevara and other matters, Castro was growing increasingly sensitive to charges that he had sold out his revolutionary principles in exchange for harmony with his Soviet providers. He also was becoming increasingly aware that the bargain he had reached with the Latin American communist parties the previous November had been extremely one-sided. In view of these factors, it is difficult to imagine how Castro could have accepted the sort of Tricontinent Conference the Soviets had in mind for him.

The Soviets, it may be assumed, conceived of the tricontinent movement in much the same terms they applied to AAPSO. They wished to have a movement strong enough to preempt the field from other competing movements which might be hostile to the U.S.S.R., but not so strong as to threaten other more direct channels of Soviet influence with the groups involved. They wished to have a group militantly leftist enough to provide useful propaganda ammunition against the West, but not so militant as to give aid and comfort to the Chinese or to commit the Soviets beyond the dictates of their better judgment.

Compared to past AAPSO conferences, the Tricontinent Conference was certainly expected to be larger and more impressive. The arithmetic of three continents versus two required it and so did Soviet plans concerning the Chinese. If the tricontinent organization was to supplant and absorb AAPSO, it had to do so almost by acclamation—it had to be seen by all (except the Chinese) as a step upward. But it is clear that the Soviets expected no qualitative change from AAPSO to a tricontinent movement. They planned to send the same sort of delegation, to say the same sort of things (with more attention to Latin America), and to oversee passage of the same sort of resolutions as at past AAPSO conferences. And they apparently expected the whole thing to attract only a little more attention in non-communist circles than past AAPSO conferences,* the last of which went virtually unnoticed outside of Moscow, Peking, and a few African capitals.

For Castro, however, the Tricontinent Conference was a very different sort of thing. For one thing it was the culmination of his long-frustrated ambition to take his place as a third-world leader alongside such previous AAPSO conference hosts as Nasser, Touré, Nyerere, and Nkrumah. For another it was a chance to break out of the political isolation which he had fallen into as a result of the missile crisis, his impotence in the Dominican crisis, and his deepening dependence on the U.S.S.R. To Castro, the success of the conference was vital for the sake of his own prestige, not because it would ensure the absorption of AAPSO. If the Chinese lost their coveted fifth AAPSO conference as a result of his conference, well and good, but he was not prepared to force a breakup of his own meeting merely to deal the Chinese the nasty blow desired by Moscow.

How much were Moscow and Castro aware of each other's real plans? How much mutual deception was involved in Soviet and Cuban preparations for the conference? Judging from the Soviet Cuban divergencies which developed at the conference itself, it appears that conscious deception was involved,

---

* This was, of course, a gross miscalculation of Latin American and U.S. sensitivities, as the Soviets rapidly learned. See below, p. 93.

mainly on the part of Castro. The deception appeared to be of fairly late origin, however, since at the September preparatory meeting in Cairo the Cubans made proposals which, if accepted, would have prevented the Tricontinent Conference from taking the Castroite line it took. The most plausible explanation of the Cuban behavior is that Castro began to realize the full possibilities of the conference only after the Cuban proposals at Cairo had been rejected and the Cubans faced the task of selecting several groups from each Latin American country to be represented on their respective "national solidarity committees."

This period of selecting national committees from Latin America, from September through December 1965, coincided exactly with the open PCV retreat from armed struggle in Venezuela and with Castro's unmistakable resentment of past concessions to the U.S.S.R. It is thus quite logical to assume that the Cuban decision to invite a large contingent of Latin Americans from groups not approved by the traditional communist parties was made in these last four months of 1965. It is also reasonable to assume that Castro himself had little idea of just how open a confrontation there would be between the pro-Moscow communists and the nonparty revolutionaries. Castro must have realized, however, that he was defying the spirit, if not the letter, of the 1964 Havana conference in some of his invitations. Wherever there were significant insurrectionist groups outside the communist parties, they were given invitations, whatever their relations with the parties. In the case of the Mexican delegation, a late December preparatory committee meeting chaired by Cubans specifically ruled against a plea by a traditional communist party for admission in lieu of the more Castro-oriented MLN.[5]

As the January 3 opening date of the Tricontinent Conference approached, the Soviets must have been plagued with many doubts about the behavior of the Cubans. Apparently they were still confident, however, that they had firm commitments from Castro to join them in thwarting Chinese designs and specifically to support the formation of a tricontinent organization with headquarters in Cairo. The Cairo site for the tricontinent headquarters was essential because any other headquarters site would give the Chinese a chance to keep a separate AAPSO going long enough to convene their Peking AAPSO conference. Conversely, the Chinese could not possibly prevent a merger, in Moscow's view, if the new organization was based in the same place as the old. Beyond these commitments, the Soviets could only keep their fingers crossed. They were willing to accept a "Chinesey" flavor to the conference resolutions as long as a resolution of their own on peaceful coexistence could pass also; they could afford to let the Chinese win minor skirmishes as long as the main organizational question was resolved in their favor.

Blowup at Havana

Once the Tricontinent Conference got under way, the divergence of Soviet and Cuban designs began to become fully apparent. At the very beginning of the conference, Castro made a move which might have forewarned the Soviets that something distasteful was in store for them: He launched an unexpected attack on the Chinese for cutting back on rice shipments to Cuba.[6] The Soviets were undoubtedly delighted at this further show of Cuban alignment with the U.S.S.R., but they should have realized they were not going to get something for nothing. Castro's move was in fact quite analogous to his earlier move toward seeming orthodoxy in renaming the Cuban party.

Immediately after rebuking the Chinese, Castro began hedging on his commitment to help Moscow establish tricontinent headquarters in Cairo. The Cubans gave maximum publicity to any statements from delegates favoring Havana as the site of a tricontinent organization, with an obvious view toward gaining a bandwagon momentum. Osmani Cienfuegos, chairman of the Cuban delegation, stated in his January 6 speech:

> Some opinions have been advanced regarding the maintenance of the Afro-Asian Solidarity Organization and the parallel creation of a tricontinental organization with [its] seat— at the suggestion of some of the delegations—in Havana. The selection of Cuba as a seat would undoubtedly be an honor to us, but our position is not conditioned by any aspirations of a nationalist nature that might create obstacles. If the Conference should decide to establish one sole organization to unify the anti-imperialist efforts of Asia, Africa, and Latin America with Cairo as a seat, Cuba would back that decision, but in this case its vote would be conditioned . . . to the designation of a representative of the heroic Vietnamese people as its president.[7]

Thus, the Cubans formally voiced support for Cairo, but in a most backhanded way, and with a condition attached which they knew would be unpalatable to other factions at the conference, notably the Africans.

After this statement, there is no indication that the Cubans felt any further obligation to work for

a Cairo seat for the new organization. The Council
of the OAS report on the conference, which contains the best available information on the internal
disputes at the Havana sessions, states that the Cubans worked intensively behind the scenes at the
beginning of the conference to line up support for a
Havana headquarters:

> At the beginning of the meeting the Latin American dele-
> gations held an important session to settle the differences be-
> tween the Communist party members who favored the [Cairo]
> proposal of the Soviet Union and the UAR (Argentines,
> Chileans, and Uruguayans, among others) and the members
> of "liberation movements" who were in favor of a separate
> Latin American organization or else of having the headquart-
> ers of the tricontinental organization in Havana (Mexicans,
> Venezuelans, Guatemalans, and Puerto Ricans, among
> others). Once again, Castro sided with the "liberation move-
> ments," and at his urging the Communist party members with-
> drew their initial support for the position of the Soviet Union
> and the UAR.[8]

The Soviets, meanwhile, were conducting their
own maneuvers to gain a merger of AAPSO with
the new tricontinent organization. First they tried to
accomplish this by relatively straightforward tactics. To quote Peking, "On the eve of the opening
of the Tricontinental Conference, the Soviet and
Indian delegates rushed up and down the Havana
Libre Hotel and tried to collect signatures demanding a meeting of the executive committee of AAPSO
in Havana."[9] When this effort lost steam because
of adamant Chinese objections, the Soviets and
their followers tried to get the conference to pass a
resolution on the "enlargement" of AAPSO into a
tricontinent organization. This effort also failed,
now apparently because of Cuban-led Latin Ameri-

can opposition. According to Peking, "Most Latin American delegates also indicated that the Tricontinent Conference could discuss only the problems concerning the establishment of a three continent agency, but it had no right to discuss problems concerning the AAPSO."[10]

The Soviet delegation was finally left with no further options. It had to demand that the new tricontinent organization be seated in Cairo, where it could absorb AAPSO at some later date. In this, however, the Soviets found themselves in direct confrontations with the Cubans. Not only were the Cubans now adamant about wanting the tricontinent Secretariat in Havana, but the Chinese had also let it be known that they would withdraw from the conference if Cairo were chosen for the headquarters. With both his own role in the new organization and the success of his conference at stake, Castro intervened personally. He espoused his views forcefully in private conversations with individual delegations, and he took the added precaution of closing the Havana airport to ensure that delegates would not leave without reaching an agreement. Finally the Soviets capitulated, but not without leaving a bitter taste in the mouths of the Cubans. Not only had the Soviets shown themselves completely insensitive to Castro's desire for the tricontinent Secretariat, but they had appeared willing to sacrifice the whole edifice of "tricontinental unity" for the sake of denying the Chinese their next AAPSO conference.

Communists versus guerrillas. On other matters at the conference, Castro's growing irritation at the behavior of the Soviets and their Latin American followers was becoming increasingly manifest. Not all of this irritation could be traced to past failures of the traditional communists to wage revolution; part undoubtedly sprang from the impression they made at the conference itself. Castro undoubtedly entered the conference with a chip on his shoulder against the traditional communists and with a resentment against the 1964 agreement which had bound him to them, but the atmosphere of the conference was bound to reinforce his prejudices. In November 1964, he had been the misfit, the naive country boy among sophisticated Marxist-Leninist revolutionaries, and he had accepted the game on their sensible and logical terms. Now at the Tricontinent Conference he and the rifle-wielding guerrillas from Venezuela, Guatemala, and Portuguese Guinea were setting the tone, and in this context the old-line communists were the ones out of place. They were aging, cautious, and pale in contrast to such guerrilla commanders as Luis Turcios of Gautemala, and their obvious discomfort at some of the ultraradical themes of the conference bespoke years of bureaucratic subservience to Moscow.

If Castro reacted to the guerrillas and party hacks at the conference in a very personal way, he also had specific disputes over resolutions and procedures to feed his grievances. Among the most heated of these concerned the resolution on Guadeloupe. The delegate from Guadeloupe, a member of the French Communist Party, advocated autonomy for the island during debates in the political committee. The Venezuelan delegation, however, demanded independence for Guadeloupe and, according to the OAS report, "a violent clash occurred between the communist party members of the Latin American delegations, supported by the

Soviets, and the Latin American members of the 'liberation movements,' supported by the Chinese." Cuba, apparently unable to bear what it must have viewed as communist support for a form of colonialism, sided with the "liberation movements" and tipped the balance in their favor.

In public statements by the Cubans during the conference, there was a visible progression toward increased militancy. The opening address by Cuban President Dorticos was far from mild in tone; it did not declare armed violence to be the rule everywhere, but only "when imperialism and reaction close the doors to the legal forms of struggle."[11] The formula in Castro's speech at the close of the conference, however, left significantly less room for legal tactics:

If . . . it is understood once and for all that sooner or later all or almost all peoples will have to take up arms to liberate themselves, then the hour of liberation for this continent will be advanced. What with the ones who theorize, and the ones who criticize those who theorize while beginning to theorize themselves, much energy and time is unfortunately lost; we believe that on this continent, in the case of all or almost all peoples, the battle will take on the most violent forms.[12]

A more worrisome part of Castro's concluding speech as far as the Soviets were concerned, however, was his new turn toward seeming communist orthodoxy in his attack on Trotskyism. Was this another disguised slap at Peking, for which the Soviets would eventually pay, or was it a screen to cover a shift toward certain aspects of Trotskyism —such as the placing of world revolution before socialist construction? According to one journalist at the conference, the Soviets were for once on their guard: "Castro has spoken for two hours and a half. A speech in many ways astounding. Even the Soviet journalists, in the row behind me, seemed puzzled. Throughout the night the head of the Soviet delegation to the conference, Anatoli Sofronov, will confer with his ambassador. Something unforeseen has happened."[13] Whatever Castro's words meant, it was clear that he was deeply sensitive to charges that he had abandoned Guevara's principles at Soviet orders. Furthermore, it seemed that he was prepared to go to some lengths to prove he had not stopped aiding revolutionaries in other countries.

Venezuela and the Question of Material Aid

In the documents of the Tricontinent Conference, just as in the more recent AAPSO documents, there is a recurrent theme which is never to be found in public statements of the established international communist fronts such as the World Peace Council and the World Federation of Democratic Youth. This is the idea that the advanced "liberated countries" such as the U.S.S.R. have a *duty* to aid "liberation movements" and newly "liberated" countries. The international fronts may, and often do, express profuse gratitude for Soviet generosity, but never in a tone which could be construed as hortatory.

The Tricontinent documents, however, contain such intriguing passages as the following:

It is the unavoidable duty of all revolutionary countries to provide *on a free basis* high-level professors and technicians

to developing countries to foster the formation of their
scientists and technicians.

     [The conference] *Demands* from all revolutionary forces
represented in the Tricontinental Conference, the intensification of their efforts so that the authentic representatives of
the countries that are fighting, weapons in hand, may receive
economic, financial, and material aid of all types, including
weapons and ammunition, to liberate their countries and con-
solidate world peace.

  .   .   .   .   .

    The conference proclaims the right and *duty* of the peo-
ples of Asia, Africa, and Latin America and of the progressive states and governments of the world, to give material
and moral support to peoples fighting for their liberation....[14]

    The implication of these and similar passages is
that Conference delegates considered it essential to
apply moral pressure on the Soviets and other developed socialist countries to get them to fulfill their
"internationalist" duties to deserving revolutionary
causes. The Cubans, in particular, concerned themselves with this matter, almost as if Castro was
beginning to see himself as a sort of revolutionary
conscience for the Soviets, forcing them to live up to
the implications of their vague statements of "solidarity and support" for liberation movements.
    The case closest to Castro's heart (except pos-
sibly Vietnam) was of course the languishing Venezuelan guerrilla movement. At the Tricontinent
Conference, Castro did everything in his power to
enhance the status of the FALN delegation and advance the cause of international aid to the Venezuelan rebels. The FALN was already in a strong posi-

tion in the tricontinent movement by being on the Latin American third of the preparatory committee, and by being the only Latin American delegation other than the Cuban one which had attended the Winneba AAPSO conference. Castro strengthened this base considerably by allowing the FLN-FALN some fifteen members on its delegation (versus around five for most of the other Latin American delegations) and by arranging for some of the meetings to be chaired by the head of the Venezuelan delegation, Pedro Medina Silva.

Although the Venezuelan delegation said nothing of the internal differences in the Venezuelan communist movement, its attitude on various questions at the conference was much closer to that of Bravo and Ojeda than that of the PCV Politburo. The Venezuelans were one of the few Latin American delegations cited by Peking as being openly opposed to the U.S.S.R. on selected votes, and before the conference the FALN delegation joined forces with the Vietnamese to pressure the conference into excluding the Yugoslavs from observer status at Havana.[15]

The main goal of the Venezuelan delegation at the conference, however, was not to irritate Moscow but to end the FALN's financial dependence on the PCV Politburo and to establish channels of outside aid flowing directly to the FALN "unified command." The conference resolution on Venezuela, pushed through by the FALN delegation with evident Cuban approval and assistance, called upon all countries to "recognize the Venezuelan National Liberation Front as the organization that leads armed struggle." The resolution also openly asked for outside aid:

> Imperialism unblushingly aids its lackeys. We consider that the peoples who struggle for their liberation also must unblushingly aid revolutionary movements such as ours. . . .
> We ask [the conference] . . . to create a special fund to aid the people who are carrying out revolutionary struggle in Latin America, especially Venezuela.[16]

The nature of the FALN demands at Havana is further clarified by excerpts from another document, apparently the speech of a Venezuelan representative at the conference, which was published in the French left-wing journal *Partisans*:

> Solidarity of the European socialist countries and those countries of our three continents where the revolutionary movements are in power, with our fighting movements, can be based only on the internal needs of these movements. . . .
> Our problem no longer is merely to fight a war. To fight a war with dynamite and machine guns or submachine guns. But the problem now is to win this war. And you can win this war only with radio stations, with thousands of submachine guns and many other weapons.[17]

The implication of this and the other statements is that past aid to the FALN has been motivated not by a desire to give it the wherewithal to take power but by other considerations. Such other considerations, of course, would have included the Soviet desire to show that revolutionary ideals had not been sacrificed to the pursuit of socialist prosperity, as well as the PCV desire to keep the FALN war simmering as a bargaining card in political maneuverings.

How much the FALN got as a result of these

pleas is difficult to guess. They did gain independent status in the newly formed tricontinent organization, AALAPSO (Afro-Asian Latin American Peoples Solidarity Organization). In addition, they were presumably in a good position to claim a share of any funds the member countries were willing to put into the tricontinent solidarity fund. The FLN was one of the four Latin American members of the Executive Secretariat of the tricontinent organization, and provided the chairman for a Tricontinental Committee of Support to the People of Vietnam. With these credentials and with the wording of the Venezuelan resolution passed by the conference, the FLN-FALN was clearly "respectable" enough in third-world revolutionary circles for Castro or anyone else to safely aid it directly without reference to the PCV position, whatever the 1964 Havana conference had said.

Getting any very substantial assistance out of the tricontinent solidarity fund was likely to be another matter, however, judging either from the precedent of the AAPSO solidarity fund or from the structure of the new organization. AAPSO's fund, even though it has been "serving" an area in which there are few communist parties to provide alternative conduits for funding revolutionaries, still has by all indications dealt with only relatively small sums of money. Where Soviet interest in African developments has been high, as in the Congo, funds have flowed through more reliably controlled channels.

In the tricontinent organization, however, the Soviet position was considerably weaker than it had been in AAPSO. At the Tricontinent Conference, Cuba and the other conference leaders had generously allowed the U.S.S.R. and Communist China to sit on the Committee of Assistance and Aid to the National Liberation Movements and of Struggle against Neocolonialism, but had pointedly excluded them from the Executive Secretariat, which is the ruling body of the organization. They were understandably miffed at this arrangement, and according to Peking they made a determined attempt to gain a seat on the Secretariat, quitting only after an unsuccessful eight-hour battle in a meeting of Asian delegation heads. In the end, the only communist countries represented on the Executive Secretariat were Cuba (as Secretary-General), North Korea, and North Vietnam (via the NFLSV). Thus the Soviets were cordially invited to write checks for the organization, but were given little direct influence over how they were to be spent. Needless to say, under such circumstances, Soviet checks were likely to be rather small. Cuba, of course, might happily contribute to the Tricontinent till, but it could just as well aid its protégés directly.

Repercussions of the Tricontinent

The impact of the Tricontinent Conference on Cuban-Soviet relations went far beyond the frictions of the conference itself. The Soviets had not merely lost; they had lost ignominiously. They had been beaten in their own game, in a game they had advertised in advance as a victory for their side over the Chinese. And it was the Cubans, the greenhorns of the communist world, who had manipulated the Soviets' own slogans to defeat them. Thus, there was added to the Cuban side of the relationship an air of braggadocio which had been absent for the fifteen months since Khrushchev's over-throw in 1964.

An adjunct of this new confidence was a tendency toward involvement in areas where the Cubans had previously been aloof. At international communist front meetings, where the Cubans had heretofore either been absent or at least relatively quiet, Cuban delegations were suddenly vociferous participants.[18] If previously Castro had dismissed the Sino-Soviet ideological squabbles as "byzantine" nonsense, he now obviously recognized them as essential parts of a game he might very well play to his own advantage. Immediately after the close of the Tricontinent Conference, Castro gathered all the Latin American delegates together and organized an AAPSO-like Latin American Solidarity Organization (LASO) to be located in Havana. LASO's first order of business was to organize the Latin American Solidarity Conference, which convened in late July 1967. Castro also immediately set out to organize a Latin American Students Conference in Havana, which was held July 9–August 11, 1966. This conference set up still another organization, the Continental Latin American Students Organization (OCLAE), with close ties to both LASO and AALAPSO.[19] Finally Castro intensified his efforts in the international communist student and youth fronts, IUS and WFDY, to get the next World Youth Festival brought to Havana.

The new Cuban posture of confident involvement in international communist politics was accompanied and assisted by a new communist alignment which was solidified, if not formed, at the Tricontinent Conference. This was the alignment of the radical have-nots of the communist world—Cuba, North

Korea, and North Vietnam—against the communist giants. Just as Cuba had been drifting away from close alignment with the U.S.S.R. in late 1965, North Korea and North Vietnam had likewise been drifting away from close association with Communist China, and at the Tricontinent Conference all three recognized the similarity of their positions. All three wished to stay independent of Moscow, but without falling into the clutches of Peking and without diminishing the amount of aid they could get from the Soviets. All three saw their external political goals threatened by any U.S.-U.S.S.R. rapprochement; all realized that strengthening their ties to Moscow would not in itself (as Cuba had most recently learned) guarantee added support to their external aims; and all saw the need for more effective ways of exerting pressure on Moscow than the decreasingly credible threat of alignment with Peking.

It was entirely logical, therefore, that Cuba, North Korea, and North Vietnam should form an axis, an entente, a claque to beat the drums for each other's causes. AALAPSO itself was the first institutional expression of their entente; they held the key positions in its Secretariat, and their causes headed the list of tricontinent goals. But in many other ways the three nations began to strengthen their mutual solidarity and coordinate their propaganda themes. Cuba and North Korea declaimed loudly on the importance of preparing to send "volunteers" to Vietnam; all exchanged high-level delegations and effusive greetings; all expounded on the importance of being faithful to proletarian internationalism and avoiding interference in the internal affairs of fraternal countries. All obviously agreed that Moscow (and perhaps also Peking) should be both more generous in aid and less demanding in obedience, and they said so as often and as openly as they dared.

A final factor introduced into the Soviet-Cuban relationship by the Tricontinent Conference was the image of the conference itself. For both emotional and pragmatic reasons, Castro wished to inflate the importance of the Trincontinent Conference as much as possible. Any criticism or denigration of the conference he took as a direct affront to Cuba, and at communist front conferences the Cubans were to be found insisting adamantly that due homage be paid the Tricontinent. So anxious was Castro that the Tricontinent be taken seriously that he stated he would attend the next Tricontinent Conference (originally scheduled for Cairo in 1968) in person.[20]

The Soviet side. By the time the Tricontinent Conference was half over, the Soviets had begun to recognize that they had miscalculated, and their propaganda media grew less avid in praise of the conference. But it was not until the conference had closed that they grasped the full extent of their miscalculation. Not only had their great investment in the meeting failed to demolish the Chinese, but it had almost completely freed Castro from his 1964 commitment to good behavior while giving him a magnificent instrument for troublemaking. The Cuban leader had been put in a mood of cocky belligerence which boded ill for Soviet interests elsewhere in the hemisphere. The Soviets were disastrously overcommitted to Castroism in Latin America, and Castro was doing everything in his power to commit them further.

In addition, the Soviets had grossly miscalculated the tolerance which the Western hemisphere governments would show toward this sort of affair. The Havana meetings were barely over when Moscow began to feel the backlash from Latin American governments incensed at the interventionist implications of the conference. Soviet diplomacy began back-pedaling as furiously (but as quietly) as possible. On February 11, 1966, after actions by Latin American governments in the OAS and the U.N. censuring and protesting the Tricontinent Conference, the U.S.S.R. circulated a *note verbale* to most of the Latin American governments (or their U.N. missions, for countries lacking diplomatic relations with the U.S.S.R.), virtually disavowing the actions of its delegation to the Tricontinent Conference: "Statements are being circulated . . . that representatives of Soviet social organizations taking part in this Conference issued calls for subversive activities in the Latin American countries, for interference in internal affairs, etc. Brazenly falsifying the facts, some spread the statement as though it were not representatives of Soviet social organizations who had taken part, but those of the Soviet government."[21]

On the very day that the U.S.S.R. made this rather meek defense, however, the U.N. Secretary-General received a belligerent letter from Fidel Castro asserting that his government (not just his "social organizations") "fully adhered" to the Tricontinent decisions. In the same letter, Castro depicted the governments which had criticised his conference as having "betrayed" their people and as "serving foreign interests."[22] With this one stroke, Castro demonstrated to Moscow that he would resent any

93

Soviet effort to play down the conference, and he picked a quarrel with the Latin American government which Moscow had been most assiduously courting for the previous year-and-a-half, that of Frei in Chile.

Moscow, however, remained determined to de-emphasize the Tricontinent Conference. The Soviet message to the Colombian Communist Party's Tenth Congress in early February 1966 mentioned nothing of the Tricontinent Conference or the armed struggle which had been its predominant theme.[23] Indeed, as 1966 wore on, the tricontinent organization often received less Soviet attention than the anachronism of AAPSO. The Cubans finally had this to say on the behavior of Moscow and its followers in Latin America:

Many friends of the Tricontinental Conference blush at its conclusions. Instead of shouting the meaning of the tri-continental discussions, they expound to the masses roads and formulas for attaining power completely divorced from the fighting conclusions of the Havana Tricontinental Conference. They describe the Tricontinental Conference as in-nocence personified. For these defenders of the conference, the important meeting of January this year was a kind of social meeting, a contest of orators, or an amiable inter-racial conference.

In fact, the Havana Tricontinental Conference was neither innocuous nor innocent![24]

VII. THE VENEZUELAN COMMUNIST SPLIT INTERNATIONALIZED

Unquestionably the Tricontinent was a major set-back in the efforts by the soft-line PCV leadership to pull the party out of armed struggle. Until the conference, they had achieved significant interna tional acceptance of their new position. In late September, the Italian communist newspaper *L'Unità* published a sympathetic description of the democratic peace line and the difficulty of halting guerrilla "adventurism." This was based on an interview with PCV Politburo member Hector Mujica. A month later, on October 26, the Yugoslavs printed a lengthy story in *Politika* documenting the unsuitability of continuing guerrilla warfare in Venezuela. And *Pravda* published an interview with imprisoned soft-line leader Jesus Faria on December 31, the very eve of the Tricontinent. Now these gains were to be seriously eroded by the publicity and prestige the Tricontinent gave the hard-liners of the FLN-FALN.

Initially the PCV reaction to the Tricontinent Conference was silence—a particularly striking silence in view of the full coverage given the conference by the noncommunist press of Caracas. Party leaders were obviously unhappy about the conference but faced enough problems without unnecessarily provoking Castro on this matter. Their attention at this point was fixed on maintaining some sort of momentum in the democratic peace campaign and trying to nip Bravo's divisionist maneuvers in the bud. A definitive PCV commentary on the Tri-

95

continent was not forthcoming until the open break between the PCV Politburo and Cuba late in the year.

Others, however, were less anxious to avoid offending Castro. The Yugoslavs, whose long-standing annoyance with the Cubans had been sharply reinforced by their exclusion from the Tricontinent Conference, printed an article in the January 24 *Borba* criticising the conference for treating the FALN so royally at a time when "according to reports from Venezuela, the leaders of the country's CP . . . have decided to break publicly with the FALN, whose tactics of guerrilla warfare they consider harmful and incorrect." In the same vein, an unidentified Venezuelan communist interviewed in Paris was quoted as saying the Tricontinent Conference had been a "disaster for the PCV." He added that the PCV members of the Venezuelan delegation to Havana had been insulted and had—with the complicity of the Cubans—been given a role secondary to the MIR in conference activities.[1]

Such allegations touched a sensitive nerve in Havana. The Cuban newspaper *Granma* on February 14 lashed back at the Yugoslavs in a lengthy editorial: "Let *Borba* know that the broad front of the real progressive and revolutionary forces of Latin America is not reached by means of hesitation before imperialism or by agreements with imperialist puppet governments, but . . . by means of revolution." On the following day the Cuban paper published a denial of the Yugoslav assertions by the PCV-FALN representative in Havana, Hector Marcano Coello.*

* Marcano's role in the Cuban-Venezuelan communist relationship appears to have been almost purely that of a

Interestingly enough, the Soviets were concerned enough over Cuban sensitivities to the Venezuelan situation that they felt it necessary to insist that *they* were not urging the PCV to break with the FALN. In a "Radio Peace and Progress" broadcast of February 18, Moscow denied London *Daily Mirror* reports that they had advised Venezuelan communists to lay down their arms and wage an exclusively legal fight: ". . . the Soviet people completely support the Venezuelan patriots' fight for freedom and independence of their country in the form chosen by Venezuelans and using the means they consider convenient and indispensable."

All of this proved only that the matter was a very touchy one, and for the next several months Moscow and Havana gave only indirect evidence of obvious differences in viewpoint toward Venezuela. In February and March the Cubans carried a series of articles by Ojeda in *Granma* and extolled Bravo in *Juventud Rebelde*, but they said nothing about their attempt to take control of the FLN-FALN.[2] A little later the Soviets gave a high-level reception to PCV soft-liner Jesus Faria on his arrival in Moscow following his release from prison in Caracas, but both he and his hosts made only the most guarded comments on the Venezuelan communist situation. Neither communist capital sought a direct confrontation, but there could be little doubt that the Cuban and Soviet positions on the general ques-

mediator, loyal to the PCV but anxious to mollify Castro. For example, he gave a Castroite flavor to the PCV line and he praised Bravo and Ojeda, but he ignored their "unified FLN-FALN command." His replacement in mid-1966 (see p. 106) was clearly of opposite loyalties.

tion of policy toward "liberation wars" were getting further apart rather than closer.

For Castro, the surrogate target of Chile provided an outlet for outrage at Soviet and orthodox communist tactics. Beginning with his March 13 speech, Castro initiated a bitter feud with the Frei government in Chile, heaping scorn on the one leader whom Moscow obviously hoped would become the de Gaulle of the OAS. ". . . if the case for Chile has really served for anything," sneered Castro on March 20, "it is not to point a new way for the revolutionary masses, but to put before all revolutionaries in the hemisphere still more forcefully, the question of whether the peaceful triumph of revolution is possible in the face of the exploiting classes. . . . Chile's experiment will serve to justify Cuba's course still further to the revolutionaries of the hemisphere."

Castro's pugnacious mood was brought to the very seat of communist bureaucratic caution at the Twenty-third Soviet Party Congress on March 31, where Cuban representative Armando Hart repeatedly reminded other delegates of the "policy of combat" proclaimed by the Tricontinent Conference and moralized that "acquiescence and passivity" would "never be the policy of revolution."[3] Other delegates, in contrast, virtually ignored the recent conference. The Cuban histrionics were among the few flaws in what was otherwise the most uniformly dull and humdrum CPSU Congress in recent history. According to Belgrade radio, Hart's comments caused a "commotion in the halls."

On May Day, Fidel himself returned to the podium and to the offensive. In an unmistakable slap at Soviet stinginess in aiding other "revolutionary peoples," Castro asserted that the Cubans would never be found building "a communism based on abundance or on superabundance" while "peoples in loincloths" waged revolution outside. On May 23, in a speech at the funeral of a Cuban soldier killed at the perimeter of Guantánamo Naval Base, Raul Castro declared that Cuba would "redouble" efforts to assist liberation movements in the "three continents." Finally in the growing polemic with the Yugoslavs over whether the Tricontinent Conference had been "sectarian," the May 8 *Granma* gave the first clear Cuban refutation of the popular front argument against guerrilla tactics:

What the Yugoslav spokesmen do not understand is that in recent years certain schematic conceptions of the methods and form of struggle have definitely undergone a crisis. In Latin America the Cuban revolution has precipitated this crisis. . . . The Cuban revolution made it clear that vigorous action—decided, valiant, and audacious—unites the masses, closes the links between the vanguard and the people, and advances the class struggle. In this way the Cuban revolution forged something more important than a 'united front.' We forged a Marxist-Leninist revolutionary vanguard around which grew unity and the strength of all the people.

The break finally came on June 11, with the publication in *Granma* of a May 30 letter to Castro from the "unified politico-military general command" of the FLN-FALN, Fabricio Ojeda, Américo Martin, and Douglas Bravo. It referred to the PCV indirectly, with the observation that "many are hesitating in the face of sacrifices and difficulties," and it justified the formation of a "real revolutionary leadership" by noting that "conciliation with imperialism and with the ruling classes . . . can only act as a brake on the popular struggle, encourage illusions among the masses, and perpetuate the exploitation and scorn suffered by our peoples." When the report of the letter was picked up by the Caracas press, the PCV and Moscow had no alternative but to face up to this blatant Cuban violation of the 1964 Havana agreements.

The Battle to Control the FALN

The Cuban publication of the letter from the dissident FALN faction in effect wrote finis to the long and ill-omened PCV effort to retain control of the FALN while denying that there was a basis for its existence. For the previous six months, while the Cubans refrained from open criticism, the PCV had tried desperately to prevent the Bravo-Ojeda dissident group from getting under way. At the time of the Tricontinent, the battle had not been completely lost—Bravo and Ojeda had only reached their agreement to start the reorganization of the FLN and FALN on December 10, three weeks before the conference, and they could not have progressed very far by January. Indeed, when the PCV Politburo met in January to call Bravo to account, he was not prepared to challenge the majority. While denying that he had engaged in any divisive activities, he agreed to PCV sanctions against one of his lieutenants, Alberto Pasquier. According to subsequent PCV statements, Pasquier had been actively lobbying on behalf of Bravo's movement among Venezuelan leftists and attempting to discredit the party leaders.[4]

Bravo's movement was apparently set back somewhat by this act of discipline, and the PCV Polit-buro exploited its advantage by issuing new state-ments concerning a popular front-style "broad political regrouping." The FALN produced no counterstatements about guerrilla actions, and at one point, even Radio Havana (March 5) quoted a PCV Politburo document stating that "the com-munists will not be an obstacle in the way of any measure sincerely intended to create an atmosphere of political relaxation." There were stories in the Caracas press of offers by guerrilla leaders to negotiate with the government for a return to civi-lian life.[5] In addition, there were signs that the PCV might be pressuring the guerrillas to abandon the hills to engage in these negotiations. This was the period when, according to later statements of the dissident FALN faction, "a series of theses emerged which entailed capitulation and [were] designed to liquidate the armed struggle in Venezuela. Efforts were even made to get the guerrillas to negotiate with the government—this was an effort to bring the guerrillas down."[6]

It is doubtful that this intensive political maneu-vering by the PCV was done in any real hope that the guerrillas would lay down their arms. The guer-rilla leaders had too much of their lives invested in the guerrilla cause to trade their guerrilla titles for any sort of peaceful anonymity. But the PCV's ef-forts did serve as an indication to the government of good faith, and the release of Jesus Faria and Domingo Alberto Rangel from prison in March was obviously related to their known opposition to continued guerrilla warfare.

If, as the PCV evidently believed, the remaining guerrillas were foredoomed in any case, there was nothing to lose in trying to negotiate in their name. Indeed, since the PCV strategy depended, in part, on the continued failure of the guerrillas to produce visible successes, some members of Bravo's faction have charged that the PCV Politburo connived to produce those defeats—not only by failing to provide assistance to the guerrillas but by actually betraying them to the government. No evidence has been shown to prove or to disprove this contention.

The stance of the PCV Politburo members gave Bravo ample pretext for intensifying his separatist activities. By early April, there was no doubt that he was doing so, using internal PCV documents to sway others away from the Politburo leadership. One of the documents he was presumably using— one of the two November 1965 letters later quoted by Fidel Castro in his March 1967 denunciation of the PCV (see page 57)—somehow came into the hands of the Caracas newspaper *La Tarde*, which published its full text on April 6. It thus became public knowledge that three leading PCV Politburo members had declared the necessity of an FALN retreat, had spoken derisively of the "anarchic-adventurist-MIR group," and had set about imposing its line on the rest of the FLN-FALN by fiat.

By April 22, Bravo and Ojeda had lined up enough support to go ahead with a formal reorganization of the FLN-FALN Supreme Command, which they presented to the PCV Politburo as a fait accompli in a letter two days later.[7] They also began negotiations to get MIR approval for their reorganization. This was finally secured in late May when Bravo and Ojeda agreed to a MIR proposal for a triumvirate FALN leadership body composed of Ojeda, Bravo, and a MIR leader (apparently Américo Martin).[8]

The PCV Politburo was predictably enraged by this maneuver, and it convened on May 18 to suspend Bravo from the Politburo and to expel his henchman, Alberto Pasquier, altogether. The Politburo declared that Bravo had "usurped the names of the FALN and FLN" in establishing a "parallel and objectively divisive center," and that his moves were illegal and invalid "since the orders of the FALN leadership can only be given by its component parties, sectors, and members." After stating this principle, however, the Politburo promptly controverted it by claiming sole right to reorganize the FLN: "The BP[Politburo] hereby ratifies the measures already adopted whereby the reorganization of the FLN-FALN shall be carried out by the BP and its Military Commission."[9]

The significant facts of the Bravo reorganization of the FLN-FALN and the PCV's counterreorganization are: 1) that even after the success of Bravo's divisionist maneuver had become obvious, the PCV ignored this chance to become disentangled from the FALN and chose instead to insist that the fragment of the FALN still loyal to the PCV was the "true" FALN; 2) that Bravo did not burn all his bridges to the established PCV leadership but remained a party member, despite his obvious inclination towards Castroism; and 3) that the subsequent communist polemics over these matters became almost less of an intra-party matter than an international dispute between Castro and the PCV—the latter backed by other traditional Latin American communist parties fearful of renewed Cuban intervention in their own party affairs. Ojeda (who died in June by apparent suicide after his capture by the Venezuelan police) was temporarily replaced in his position as chairman of the FLN by Pedro Medina Silva, head of the Venezuelan delegation at the Tricontintent Conference.

Cuba's Intervention

Cuban involvement with the dissident movement of Bravo and Ojeda obviously did not begin with the publication of the May 30 letter, but little evidence is available on earlier Cuban behavior. One document, a June 15 letter from Bravo to Ojeda which was made public in August, provides interesting insight into the matter:

My interest in talking to you is basically associated with my desire to examine the foreign problem in detail. We are in urgent need of money, to be specific, eight thousand bolivars. It is of vital importance to organize the outside service at once. The cs. [sic, comrades?] report that they held a meeting there with the representatives of the MIR and the cs. in the host country. They reached an agreement about the constitution of the command. I answered them by telling them that those were our prerogatives here. . . . We should write to them explaining this aspect in detail, since in the long run it may become a law and both we and they may be harmed. . . .

The important thing is that their activities are salutary but they should not overstep themselves. The matter of the letter is all right, but the business of the distribution of posts is extremely dangerous.[10]

One other document is also relevant; this is a portion of Ojeda's June 6 letter to Castro which Castro failed to read in his March 1967 revelations about the PCV. After the portion cited on page 60 where Ojeda explained past PCV control over finances, he added:

> We are therefore urgently in need of help in this aspect. It must be direct assistance so that the new leadership bodies can fulfill their duties appropriately and at once. At the same time, we must strengthen the finances of the different military units, so as to enable them to solve urgent problems of maintenance and development. This is of greatest and most vital importance, since we have absolutely no funds whatsoever for the purpose.[11]

From these two quotations it would appear that around the time of the "reorganization" of the FLN-FALN, Castro had been taking an active interest (too active for Bravo's taste) in facilitating the reorganization, but still had remained reluctant to provide funds. Bravo's comment that the "outside service" needs to be organized and Ojeda's admonition that financing be "direct" seem to suggest that there were no reliable channels for funds that weren't Moscow- or PCV-dominated. This is plausible, since the Italian Communist Party, which had apparently been the vehicle for funding the PCV at the time of the Beltramini affair, had since expressed support for the PCV soft line and would hardly have been sympathetic to a Cuban attempt to circumvent the PCV. Another explanation for Cuba's apparent failure to send funds is simply caution—a recognition that this was a step not to be lightly undertaken, certainly not before the reorganization had proved successful. This, however, seems less likely in view of Castro's 1966 mood and his subsequent almost reckless defiance of Moscow and the PCV on this question.

The June pleas for help do seem to have prompted —or coincided with—a Cuban initiative to help the

Bravo group, as well as an apparent first step toward organizing an "outside service." In the latter category was the replacement, on June 27, of PCV-FLN representative in Havana, Hector Marcano Coello, by "Captain" Leonardo Quintana. The direction of Quintana's allegiance was clarified immediately after his installation, when he heaped praise on the newly formed "General Headquarters of the FLN-FALN."[12] The "direct aid" appeared to have materialized when the Venezuelan papers suddenly announced on July 27 that some twenty bearded and uniformed men had landed in two launches on the coast of Venezuela's Falcon state.

"Operation Simon Bolivar." This "guerrilla landing" was at least two-thirds a propaganda stunt, in the best (or worst) Castroite tradition. Yet there obviously had been a landing, and it was just the sort of "direct aid" which Castro would have been inclined to give in response to the June requests. According to subsequent, rather boastful, accounts of the landing by FALN participants interviewed in the Mexican magazine *Sucesos* (much of which was broadcast by Radio Havana or excerpted in *Granma*), the landing was made on July 24 by a group of Venezuelan guerrillas who had gathered on the island of Margarita earlier in the month after spending the previous two years studying guerrilla movements elsewhere (particularly in Vietnam). The idea of the landing was the obvious one: to give Bravo's forces a shot in the arm and to prove "the falsity of claims made by the oligarchy and its pseudorevolutionary sycophants that the Venezuelan revolution is demoralized and has been annihilated."[13] (The "pseudorevolutionary sycophants" are, of course, the PCV Politburo.)

Cuban-PCV Polemics Escalate

Corresponding to this manifest Cuban involvement on the side of the dissidents in the PCV-Bravo dispute was an unmistakable Cuban drift toward open renunciation (not merely violation) of the 1964 Havana accords. In Castro's July 26 speech, the Cuban leader struck out derisively at the established communist parties of Latin America, terming them "pseudorevolutionaries" and "charlatans" who constitute the "most important allies of imperialism in Latin America."

Faced with reverses, the pseudorevolutionaries proclaim the failure of the true revolutionary path. There are some who attempt to present us as war fanatics, as armed struggle maniacs. There are those who, posing as sensible people, as did many of those whom we used to know here, preach the path of electioneering charlatanism. . . .

. . . this thing about the consciousness having to come first and the struggle later is an error! The struggle has to come first, and inevitably, after the struggle, with growing impetus, comes revolutionary consciousness! . . . We would have been in a nice fix if to make a socialist revolution we had to catechise everyone with socialism and Marxism beforehand.

If the denigration of the communist parties was clear in this statement, it was still more explicit in Castro's August 29 speech:

The party . . . has broad connections with all leftwing organizations. This is consistent with the Second Havana Declaration. . . . Whether it is called a party or not, the essence lies in the contents and not in the bottle. . . .

Who will wage the revolution in Latin America? . . . The revolutionaries, with or without parties.

The PCV reaction to this growing barrage was cautious. The tone of the initial responses to Cuban support for the FALN dissidents was reproachful, as if by underplaying the Cuban misdeeds they (or Moscow) might be able to persuade Castro to return to the fold. The PCV newspaper *¿Qué?* in its issue of June 24 roundly condemned the signers of the May 30 letter to Castro but exonerated the Cubans:

> We sincerely believe that the Cuban comrades have published the aforementioned letter in good faith and in the belief that it is the result of a joint action of the Venezuelan revolutionary movement . . . the norms of solidarity, fraternity, and mutual respect that have always characterized relations between the Cuban CP and ours, make us believe that the divisionists will no longer be able to avail themselves of the pages of the official organ of the Cuban CP nor other means of publication, for their activities.[14]

As the summer progressed and it became obvious that Castro was ignoring their veiled protests, PCV leaders began expressing their pique more openly, making comments about outside meddling in their affairs and attempts to impose the Cuban revolutionary model on other parties. Toward the end of August, they finally sent a formal protest to Castro, explaining that all formulas of conciliation with the Cuban CP had been exhausted. According to a copy of the letter which reached the Caracas press in early September, the PCV Politburo accused the Cubans of giving open support to Venezuelan "anti-party" groups, of displacing the legitimate PCV representatives in the Tricontinent and Latin American solidarity organizations, and of accepting a "seditious" delegation of the FALN (presumably

Quintana *et al.*). Finally, as the compelling reason why the Cubans were obligated to stop these actions, the Politburo invoked the 1964 Havana conference:

> There can be no justification for such decisions . . . for those of us who have struggled effectively alongside you— before and after the Conference of Latin American Parties in November 1964—for the unity of the world communist movement . . . and therefore for the explicit condemnation of factionalism in all its varieties, , , , At that historic conference . . . precise standards of conduct were stipulated for the fraternal exchange between the various Communist and Workers parties of Latin American. . . . [Y]our attitude . . . obviously contradicts these standards, which we then considered—and continue to consider today— as obligatory for all.
> Relations between revolutionaries in different countries must be maintained, fundamentally, between the Communist Parties. . . .[15]

The PCV itself did not publish its views in terms this harsh until after an appropriate waiting period, perhaps to show that it was giving Castro a chance to respond. Then, on September 23, the PCV leaders lashed out publicly in their own newspaper against the Venezuelan "fractionalists" and called upon the Cuban communists "to clear up all this confusion which the anti-party groups all over Latin America are using in order to try to disqualify the communist party." They insisted there was no parallel between Castro's revolution and the situation in Venezuela and pointed out that decisions on Venezuelan communist policy and personnel could be made only in Venezuela. Finally, they hinted broadly that Castro and his Venezuelan followers were guilty of an "infantilism," "emotionalism," and "impulsiveness" which the PCV had outgrown, and they referred to the Tricontinent Conference as a "farce . . . where 'unity' was cooked up from topside and outwardly only."[16]

For the next two months the Cuban-PCV exchanges grew progressively more bitter. Castro did not reply directly to PCV protests, but Cuban media carried ever more tendentious statements by representatives of the FALN dissidents. A peak, of sorts, was reached in early December, when the Mexican magazine *Sucesos* began publishing a series of reports on the Venezuelan guerrillas, authored by the magazine's editor, Mario Menendez Rodriguez. *Sucesos* had at best a rather limited circulation, even in Mexico, but the Cubans ensured wide dissemination for its more interesting sections by broadcasting lengthy excerpts of the articles in radio programs to Latin America. If this were not enough to make one suspect that the whole *Sucesos* series was a Cuban-sponsored operation, it soon became known that Menendez was the brother of Luis Gomez-Wanguemert, editor of the Cuban newspaper *El Mundo*.[17]

The *Sucesos* articles were a full exposition of the dissident FALN case against the PCV, phrased in the harshest possible terms. The first of the articles, as quoted by Radio Havana, accused the PCV of committing "sabotage" against the armed struggle, of using "blackmail against the guerrillas," and of attempting to "capture" and "murder" Douglas Bravo. On the PCV direction of the guerrilla operations, Menendez said:

Without any faith in armed guerrilla action, without being competent to direct it, these leaders nonetheless felt that their shock troops in the mountains, obeying orders issued from the city, could serve political maneuvers, compromise scheming, a military coup that would enable them to climb to power rather than win it through real revolutionary armed battle. Now they would order an immediate attack by the guerrilla fronts, and again they would for opportunistic reasons arrange a ceasefire, a complete cessation of operations, absolute inertia on the part of fighting men, or withdrawal. . . .

What is more, since they had absolute control over finances, propaganda media, and supplies of clothing, food, and war equipment, they used blackmail against the guerrillas. When the commander of some front failed to obey the ceasefire order, they cut back on his supplies or sent him nothing at all, as happened in the case of the José Leonardo Chirinos front, commanded by the indomitable Douglas Bravo.[18]

Significantly, the harshest words of the *Sucesos* series were these, written not by FALN leaders but by editor Menendez himself. The "indomitable" Douglas Bravo, whose lengthy interview with Menendez took up the next two installments of the series, was much more discreet. He spoke of "errors," "deviations," and "regrettable mistakes," rather than treachery, and he indicated that the main reason for past FALN failures had been weakness in strategic thinking rather than PCV perfidiousness. Specifically, he said that the FALN failure to disrupt the 1963 elections had been the result of a "short-range, 'coupist' policy" and an error of strategy which expended the main FALN forces too soon. And the main subsequent error, according to Bravo, was the attempt to lead the guerrilla movement from the cities, rather than the hills. For the future, Bravo advanced a program almost indistinguishable from the PCV program prior to the democratic peace deviation. There was the same call for the "broad front" of "revolutionary and patriotic segments," including even individuals participating in the Leoni government. There was a call for both armed and unarmed struggle, both legal and illegal tactics, and there was even a warning against the "mistake of pure leftism": ". . . we must issue a warning in order not to fall into the mistakes to which we referred earlier. We must not launch our principal troops, our main forces, unless there is a favorable opportunity."[19]

The implication of the *Sucesos* series as a whole was that this was more of a Cuban, rather than a FALN initiative, that Castro was much more anxious to demonstrate the "pseudorevolutionary" character of the Latin American communist parties than Bravo. Castro's obsession with winning his debate with the PCV was increasingly obvious. It received its ultimate expression in a speech by Castro himself, his March 13 address commemorating the tenth anniversary of his 1957 attack on the Cuban presidential palace.

Castro's March 13 speech. The event which prompted Castro's personal involvement, in public, on questions of the Venezuelan revolutionary movement was the kidnap and murder of Dr. Julio Iribarren Borges, former Venezuelan social security director and brother of the Venezuelan Foreign Minister. In a statement published in the March 6 *Granma*, a member of the dissident FALN faction in Cuba publicly claimed FALN "credit" for the killing. The PCV, in contrast, had condemned the murder and publicly expressed regret that the Cuban party organ had lent its columns to such "nonsense" as this statement by a "fractionalist" and "adventurer" who had been expelled from the PCV.[20]

When Castro discussed the killing itself, he agreed with the PCV that such deeds were to be avoided by revolutionaries. But before stating this view, he delivered one of the more extraordinary denunciations of a "fraternal" communist party in the turbulent history of the world communist movement. Several of Castro's more explicit revelations about the PCV's errors and efforts to "liquidate" the Venezuelan armed struggle have been cited earlier. In addition to these, Castro drew a broader picture which clearly suggested at least tacit PCV and Soviet collaboration with the Leoni government to terminate guerrilla activities in return for "democratic legality" for the PCV and diplomatic relations for the U.S.S.R. He climaxed this harangue with an outright rejection of the terms of the November 1964 Havana agreements:

> In the name of what principles, what reasons, what revolutionary essentials were we obliged to declare the [PCV] defeatists right. . .? In the name of Marxism—Leninism? No! . . . In the name of the international Communist movement? Were we perchance obligated by the fact that it was the leadership of a Communist party? Is that perchance the idea we must have of the international Communist movement? For us the international Communist movement is, first, just that: a movement of Communists, a movement of revolutionary fighters; and whoever is not a revolutionary fighter cannot be called a Communist. . . .
> The international Communist movement as we conceive it is not a church; it is not a religious or Masonic sect that obliges us to sanctify weakness, to sanctify deviation, to pursue a policy of making bosom friends of every kind of reformist and pseudorevolutionary. . . . If in any nation those who call themselves Communists do not know how to fulfill their duty, we will support those who—even though they do not call themselves Communists—behave like real

Communists in the struggle. . . . What defines a Communist is, . . . in this continent, action in the armed revolutionary movement. . . .

Castro concluded with a vehement assertion of Cuba's ideological independence from Moscow: "This revolution will maintain its absolutely, independent position, . . . will pursue its own line, . . . will never be anyone's satellite or be subjected to anyone's conditions, and . . . will never ask anyone's permission to maintain its posture, be it in ideology or in domestic or foreign affairs."

Moscow and the Cuban-PCV Polemic

It was apparent from both the March 13 speech and Castro's speech of August 29, 1966 that he was feeling the opprobrium of Moscow-line communists for his misbehavior. In his August 1966 speech, Castro said he had been accused of "heresy," of "wanting to implement the Cuban formula mechanically," of not knowing the "role of the party." But, he answered, "What do we whom they call petty bourgeois, subjectivists, heretics care? . . . Let them condemn, criticize, and excommunicate us!" Castro's March 13 speech was almost entirely a defense against communist attacks on his attitude toward the Venezuelan revolution, but he was also more explicit than previously: "For the past several months, in the clandestine and semiclandestine press, including the legal press of that nation, and at various international events, the rightist leadership of the PCV has been levying similar imputations [similar to those of the Venezuelan Government] against our party."

Clearly Castro was under attack by friends of the PCV, as well as by the PCV, but there was no suggestion that Moscow was directly involved, except perhaps for the intriguing reference to possible "excommunication." Moscow in fact was being very discreet about the whole issue, at least to all appearances. Indeed, one suspects that their very discretion must have been as irritating to Castro as the fact of their disagreement with him. Soviet spokesman themselves avoided comment on the Venezuelan communist movement, and PCV representatives in the U.S.S.R. obviously were not granted permission to carry on their polemic in Soviet media. In September, the U.S. communist newspaper, *The Worker*, published a report on a meeting in Moscow between Gus Hall and Jesus Faria which said that the latter "was critical of outside influence on the party and pointed out how some persons in Cuba had used Cuban prestige to issue directives to Venezuela."[21] Nothing comparable appeared in the Soviet press, however.

Nonetheless the Soviets continued to demonstrate their general stance on such matters. While *Pravda* on July 29 devoted a scant five paragraphs to Castro's militant July 26 speech (thus neatly illustrating Castro's complaint in the speech that "there are friends of the revolution who publish some speeches and do not publish others), a day or so later they published a lengthy Peruvian Communist Party statement which followed the popular front theme and asserted that a revolutionary situation had not yet developed in the country.[22] Likewise in other pro-Moscow communist publications, such as, the *World Marxist Review*, the prevailing themes were the same as in 1965 : broad fronts, democratic slogans, and patience on the question of armed struggle.[23]

The Latin American CP's. Although Moscow was still not prepared to confront Castro over his Venezuelan meddling, the PCV's brother parties in Latin America were not all willing to be as reticent. For many, the PCV's experience was an ominous precedent which could all too easily be repeated in their own countries. For almost all, there was the worry that Cuba's potential for mischief would be multiplied if the Cuban-FALN predominance in the nascent Latin American Solidarity Organization went unchallenged. And for at least one party, the Colombian CP, there was reason to fear that Cuban-instigated guerrilla activities could put the kibosh on plans by the government in power to expand relations with the U.S.S.R.

The Mexican CP also, had particular reason to side openly with the PCV and seek concerted action to stop Castro's new thrust outward. This party had lost out to the more Castroite MLN (National Liberation Movement) at the Tricontinent Conference and could expect similar treatment in LASO. It was a Mexican CP initiative, apparently, that resulted in the first sign of coordinated Latin American Communist action to deal with the Castro problem. This initiative took the form of a meeting in Colombia in late October 1966 between Mexican and Colombian communist party central committee members. The communiqué of this meeting, summarized by *Pravda* on November 2, dwelt at some length on imperialism, Vietnam, and Chinese wickedness, but its main focus was obviously the Cuban problem. Specifically, the communiqué resurrected the 1964 Havana conference decisions, "ratified" them anew, and stated that the two-party conversations "demonstrated the need to continue working to apply the agreements of that conference." In addition, the communiqué specifically addressed the question of "Latin American revolutionary solidarity," and while it mentioned the Tricontinent Conference in this context, it did not mention LASO. Instead, it asserted:

> It is the conviction of the two parties that the solidarity and unity of action of the Communist parties can broadly develop on the basis of the principles established in common agreement at the (1964) Conference of the Communist Parties of Latin America. The point of departure for this solidarity is mutual respect and recognition of the independence of each party to decide in its own country the tactic it poses to the National Revolutionary Forces in accordance with the particular conditions in which the revolutionary process is developing. . . . All fractional activity, whatever its nature or origin, should be repudiated.

In addition, the two parties asserted what appeared to be a restatement of the Togliatti thesis: "The two parties . . . consider it necessary to continue to apply the forms of 'rapprochement' and cohesion elaborated by the experience of the Marxist-Leninist parties: the exchange of experiences, the realization of bilateral and regional meetings. . . ."[24]

Whether another meeting along the lines of Havana 1964 was in the offing was uncertain. The key ingredient of 1964—Moscow's need to pry Castro away from Peking—was no longer present, but now at least two of the Latin American communist parties were again gesturing in that direction.

The Mexican CP became the chief defender of the PCV against the attacks printed in *Sucesos*. Beginning with the December 15 issue of *Política*, the

Mexican communists began publicizing letters from Mexican and Venezuelan leftist leaders protesting Menendez' allegations against the PCV. One of these letters, written by PCV leader Teodoro Petkoff, observed acidly that Menendez had come "already paid to write a series not so much favoring Douglas Bravo and his followers, but slandering the PCV and its leaders," and charged that the *Sucesos* revelations had given the Venezuelan government information dangerous to the safety of several PCV leaders.[25]

The Many Loose Ends

By March 1967, the various aspects of the Venezuelan communist picture remained far from static. The degree of harmony between the Bravo-FALN dissidents and Cuba was by no means certain, despite lavish Cuban praise for Bravo. There had also been no indication of the extent or manner of any Soviet efforts to assist the PCV in strengthening its position within the Venezuelan far left. One event of early 1967 left several intriguing question marks, including the apparent defection of former Bravo-supporters Pedro Medina Silva and Pedro Vegas Castejon to the PCV side. The former, who had headed the FALN delegation to the Tricontinent Conference and was named to the dissident FALN triumvirate after Fabricio Ojeda's death, was the author of a letter to the Cuban Communist Party published in the February 14 *Política*. In this letter, Medina Silva denounced the "treacherous" "fractionalist group" of the dissident FALN, informed the Cubans that he had been named "Commanding General" of the true FALN, and announced that under his leadership the armed struggle would be "directed by Venezuelans" and would apply "the tactics and the strategy suited to the Venezuelan situation." Something had happened to change Medina's allegiance, but there was no immediate answer as to whether he had been frustrated by Cuban attempts to control the dissident FALN, had a falling out with Bravo, had been bought by the Soviets, or whether the PCV had found new funds to support guerrilla operations even while continuing the democratic peace line.

Whatever the outcome of the battle for control of the Venezuelan far left, the record of the previous three years sufficiently revealed the manner of thinking and patterns of behavior of the main protagonists. It also seemed completely certain that there could be no reversion to the Soviet-Cuban harmony over strategy in Latin America which prevailed during the first eight or nine months of 1965. Castro could never again claim naiveté about Soviet (or Chinese) declarations on world revolution, and the Soviets were unlikely to entrust Castro—even at his most contrite—with any delicate or expensive missions on their behalf.

THE COMPETING SOVIET AND CUBAN REVOLUTIONARY DOCTRINES

Castro and the Fidelista Guerrillas

From the alternating periods of convergence and divergence in Soviet and Cuban positions on Latin American revolution over the past several years, one could almost conclude that there was some sort of natural, cyclical rhythm involved, a rhythm based on such recurring factors as sugar harvests, annual economic agreements, and the mutual antipathy stored up by each side during periods of enforced harmony. Certainly there would be some validity in such an analysis, and much unnecessary excitement over new "trends" in the Soviet-Cuban relationship could be avoided by keeping these recurring factors permanently in mind. But to concentrate only on these factors would obscure a very definite and probably irreversible evolution in Cuban thinking toward the interrelated questions of Latin American revolution and the international communist movement.

At the beginning of the period under study, Castro's outlook was relatively non-ideological, almost anti-ideological. He wanted violent revolution in the rest of the hemisphere, but he did not particularly care whether or not it was conducted by the communist parties; he tended to sympathize with the Chinese in the Sino-Soviet dispute, but he had no sympathy for the Byzantine hair-splitting which formed the bulk of the polemic. Castro was, and wished to remain, a man of flamboyant action and of voluminous, imprecise, and unrehearsed speech. As Theodore Draper has observed in his analysis of Castroism, Castro always "had a deep, persistent feeling of intellectual inadequacy and inferiority, a tendency to depend on others for fundamental values or systematic thinking. . . ."[1] Until early 1965, Castro's "systematic thinker" had been Che Guevara. The Guevara legacy in the field of Latin American revolution, however, was little more than the postulate of armed struggle as a near-absolute and a how-to-do-it handbook for guerrilla warriors. Guevara's works were of little use to Castro as he single-handedly sought to refute the practiced dialecticians of the Soviet line as they lucidly explained how new events required them to behave just as they always had done.

As soon as Guevara's eclipse within Cuba became firmly established, Cuba-watchers began asking the obvious question: Who would replace him as chief ideologist? The answer, it now appears, was the young French Marxist, Régis Debray, who first visited Cuba in 1961 and returned in late 1965 to spend over a year in close contact with the Cuban leader. It is unlikely that he influenced Castro quite as much as Che Guevara had, but there can be little doubt that he helped Castro clarify his thoughts on the question of Latin American revolution, and that he transcribed them into sophisticated Marxist terminology. It is interesting to speculate that the reassertion of theoretical Castroism in Castro's speeches of July 1966, August 1966, and March 1967 were in part a result of Debray's systematic elaboration of Castroite doctrine. In any event, Debray's book, *Revolution within the Revolution*, was published in 100,000 copies amid considerable fanfare by the Cuban Casa de las Américas in January 1967.[2] From all appearances, it represents a complete and authoritative statement of Castroite revolutionary doctrine as of the end of 1966.

The Debray Book

Revolution within the Revolution is not basically an ideological work any more than Guevara's *Guerrilla Warfare* was. Debray starts with one or two basic assumptions—that Castro's regime and the Latin American "oligarchies" represent good and evil respectively, that overthrowing the existing governments (whatever their nature) in the shortest possible time should be the only goal of true revolutionaries—and then he proceeds to construct a logically consistent guerrilla warfare solution to this specific problem of power. For the most part Debray is dispassionate. In contrast to doctrinal statements by persons within the Cuban leadership, Debray's book contains few emotional attacks on the U.S.;* nor are there the usual obvious circumlocutions on matters involving the U.S.S.R. and the traditional communist parties. Only in his basic black-white premises regarding Fidel and the "oligarchies," and in his romantic faith in the purifying effects of the guerrilla life does he lapse markedly from the rigorous intellectual standards of his *Ecole Normale* background.

The focus of Debray's book is not on the question

---

* Debray even acknowledges that some Peace Corpsmen are "hard workers with patience and true abnegation," contrasting this with the lack of rural political work by domestic leftist organizations in Latin American countries (p. 30).

of "armed struggle" versus "peaceful transition to socialism," despite the fact that Debray obviously dismisses the latter thesis as absurd. The effect, if not the intent, of Debray's analysis is to bypass the "honest" revisionists such as those in Chile, Uruguay, and Costa Rica, who openly assert that armed struggle is unsuited to their countries. His heaviest criticism is directed toward those groping for a middle path between this "peaceful transition" stance and total commitment to long-term guerrilla warfare (i.e., where communist parties have tried to preempt Castroite ground). Debray lists three "old political concepts which are today, outworn, discredited, corroded by failure": 1) "the old theory of the alliance of four classes, including the national bourgeoisie"; 2) "the concept of a 'national democracy' "; and 3) "contempt for or underestimation of the peasantry" (p. 87). He does not suggest that these concepts must be defeated everywhere; his point is that the lingering influence of these concepts in such countries as Colombia and Venezuela makes it impossible for the established communist parties to carry out correct guerrilla warfare even where they have acknowledged the need for "armed struggle."

The flow of Debray's reasoning is best shown in the following series of quotations:

> For reasons beyond their control, many Latin American Communist parties made a false start, 30 or 40 years ago. . . . (p. 104)

> The phrase "armed struggle" is brandished, repeated endlessly on paper, in programs, but the use of the phrase cannot conceal the fact that in many places the *determination* to carry out the armed struggle and the *positive* definition of a corresponding strategy are still lacking. (p. 87)

To subordinate the guerrilla group strategically and tactically to a party that has not radically changed its normal peacetime organization, or to treat it as one more ramification of party activity brings in its wake a series of fatal military errors. . . . (p. 67)

. . . the force of tradition, the deep-rooted adherence to forms of organization fixed and hallowed by time, prevents the dissolution of an established structure and the passage to a new form of struggle required by the war situation. . . . In every case attempts will be made to enjoy the advantages of all forms of struggle without the drawbacks of any, to refuse to select one form of struggle as fundamental and another as subordinate. . . . This abstract policy, reformist or disoriented, converts the revolutionary movement into a disjointed marionette. In a war situation, a wrong turn by the top leadership can lead to other wrong turns, in the opposite direction, by the two wings of the armed sector: legalist yearnings of the political leadership are matched in the armed sector by uncontrolled terrorism in the city and banditry in the countryside. (pp. 74–75)

The baneful influence of the city. Debray goes into great detail in demonstrating that the traditional communist parties cannot lead a successful guerrilla war primarily because they remain tied to the city. This fact results in a host of difficulties, says Debray, any one of which can be fatal to the guerrilla movement. One of these difficulties is the lack of security suffered by guerrilla leaders. "If it remains in the cities, the political leadership will inevitably be destroyed or dismantled," writes Debray, while guerrilla commanders, forced to come down from the mountains to participate in leadership discussions, undergo "a fatal risk" (p. 68). Even if urban leaders could maintain security and avoid imprisonment, which they cannot, says Debray, they would still lack a "profound and detailed tactical understanding of military problems." "Political leadership without this knowledge cannot draft military plans alone, according to its own convenience, as support for a policy of maneuvering or bringing pressures against the bourgeois regime, and then transmit them to its military apparatus 'for implementation' " (p. 73).

In addition to these strategic and logistic problems, Debray points to several human difficulties, such as guerrilla dependency, which make it impossible to direct a guerrilla war from the cities. The guerrilla who must depend on aid and instructions from the cities becomes "gradually more of a victim of the mirage of imminent outside aid," develops an "inferiority complex," and loses sight of his "moral and political principles" (p. 70). Another human problem is that of urban embourgeoisment. Living conditions in the city inevitably breed bourgeois thinking habits among communists, causing them to forget the urgency of guerrilla material needs and to become seduced by the attractions of traditional political maneuvering, "amnesty campaigns," and international "globe-trotting." The urban-rural differences, states Debray, are so universal and deep-rooted among Latin American revolutionaries, that the "disharmony and disagreement between the mountain and the plains forces" has "the force of law."[3]

The organizational obsolescence. Besides the urban character of traditional communist parties, another major reason for their inability to direct guerrilla warfare is their adherence to traditional forms of organization. None of these make sense in a guerrilla context, states Debray. He takes fundamental issue with the sacrosanct communist organizational principle, defended by Lenin, Mao, and Ho Chi Minh alike, that politics should direct the gun, that the military must remain subordinate to the party. This principle is not valid in Latin American guerrilla warfare, Debray declares, because in contrast to China and Vietnam the existing parties of the hemisphere were not "linked from birth" with the armed struggle. Finally, the principle itself sets up a false dichotomy which fails to take into account the basically political nature of guerrilla warfare itself. "A guerrilla force cannot develop in a military sense unless it becomes a political vanguard," he asserts, and thus it is an "absurd distinction" which some communists make between "politicians" and "military" men (p. 90).

Related to this one organizational principle are several others, including bureaucratic structures, political commissars, and mass fronts. The "plethora of commissions, secretariats, congresses, conferences, mass gatherings, plenary sessions, meetings and assemblies on all levels," states Debray, is "paralyzing at best, catastrophic at worst." They can lead only to discord, a "loss of faith in the command," and a loosening of discipline, plus a "preference for organizational matters over operational tasks" (pp. 102, 115). Furthermore, the traditional communist system of political commissars to advise military contingents, states Debray, is based on the false belief that theoretical training by the party or the socialist countries creates greater political reliability than the lessons of guerrilla combat. On the contrary, he asserts, the Cuban example demonstrates that "in guerrilla warfare the fighters are trained politically more quickly and more profoundly" than in cadre schools, and it is "only the guerrilla movement" that can "guarantee that the people's power will not be perverted after victory" (pp. 89, 109). The implications of this point for existing and future revolutions led by non-guerrilla party men are vast.

Finally, Debray demolishes the one structure that communists have traditionally used for involvement in armed actions, the FLN-style political front as it existed prior to Bravo's "reorganization." Debray says that in establishing an "artifical," "improvised," "ghost" front, with a prestigious "independent personality" at the top as a figurehead, energy is diverted from the main task of constructing a people's army. "No political front, which is basically a deliberative body, can assume leadership of a peoples war," because any "composite national front is by nature disposed to political disagreements, discussions, endless deliberations, and temporary compromises" (p. 86). Efforts to hold such fronts together —what Debray terms the "unity at all costs" obsession—are futile and immobilizing at the start of guerrilla warfare, while as the guerrilla movement develops they become unnecessary. Thus, Debray disposes of the standard communist device for squeezing armed struggle into the popular front framework.

The Venezuelan ingredient. The Venezuelan communist attempt to carry on armed struggle was the most important prototype of all the behavior patterns Debray describes and condemns. It was the PCV leadership which failed to go to the mountains, which found its best leaders incarcerated, and which found its second-echelon leaders ill-equipped to lead either the party or the armed struggle (pp. 73–75). It was the FALN commanders who risked capture and death to come to the cities for political discussions in a situation "when organs break up and others form without [the guerrilla commander] being consulted" (p. 68). It was the PCV which most openly invoked traditional doctrines on political supremacy over the military in an attempt to discredit Castroite dissident activities.[4] Often Debray is explicit:

> Elsewhere [Venezuela] the number of guerrilla *focos* suddenly increased after 1962; this was an artificial growth that did not correspond to a real growth of the guerrilla movement nor of its offensive capacity. In fact, this forced growth —cause and effect of the absence of a single command— weakened the guerrillas.

> This delay can be deliberate; that is, new guerrilla fronts can be created in order to hinder the establishment of a single leadership. But in this case . . . they are not intended to wage war but to maintain a reserve of political personnel and to make propaganda for their promoters. To have a guerrilla force gives prestige. (pp. 79–90)

At other points he leaves identification to the reader:

> . . . the importance of a radio transmitter at the disposition of the guerrilla forces. The radio permits headquarters to establish daily contact with the population residing outside the zone of operations. . . . In short, radio produces a qualitative change in the guerrilla movement. This explains the muffled or open resistance which certain party leaders offer today to the guerrilla movement's use of this propaganda medium.* (pp. 108–9)

The Castro-Debray formula. If the PCV epitomized for Debray everything which had to be swept into the "dustbin of history" in order to get on

*It will be recalled that the FALN representative at the Tricontinent Conference apparently asked for radio stations, see above, p. 87.

with revolution, the Bravo-led dissident FALN was
in large measure the prototype for the new movements which he hoped could develop, with Cuban
encouragement, from the shambles of the discredited
communist parties. The central element in Debray's
formula is the unified "politico-military leadership"
located in a rural guerrilla "vanguard" organization.
This is precisely what Bravo and Ojeda set out to
create in Venezuela, and Debray specifically cites
the Venezuelan case and that of the Guatemalan
FAR as proof that the Cuban pattern of politico-
military relations was no "unique and unusual coincidence." These two examples, state Debray, confirm
and reinforce the fact that no less than a "decisive
contribution to international revolutionary experience
and Marxism-Leninism" has been made (p. 106).

Debray defines this politico-military leadership at
the outset of his book as a "strategic mobile force,
the nucleus of the People's Army and of the future
socialist state." In this definition it can be seen that
the whole question of class alliances, so fundamental
to communist thinking from Lenin to Mao, has been
firmly buried; it has been made part of the definition of a "strategic mobile force." Why is the guerrilla movement justified in assuming both political
and military command, asks Debray rhetorically?
The justification, he replies, is in "that class alliance
which it alone can achieve, the alliance that will take
and administer power, the alliance whose interests
are those of socialism—the alliance between workers and peasants. The guerrilla army is a confirmation in action of this alliance; it is the *personification*
of it" (p. 109, emphasis supplied).

Debray waxes almost mystical in his explanation
of how the guerrillas acquire the proper ideological

outlook. Socialist theory and proletarian internationalism seem to spring full-blown into the minds of assorted peasants, students, and workers as they struggle together in the mountains: "Under these conditions class egoism does not long endure. Petty bourgeois psychology melts like snow under the summer sun, undermining the ideology of the same stratum . . . By the same token, the only conceivable line for a guerrilla group to adopt is the 'mass line'; it can live only with their support, in daily contact with them. Bureaucratic faintheartedness becomes irrelevant. Is this not the best education for a future socialist leader or cadre?" (p. 111). He concludes his analysis with the logical consequence of these assertions: *"The people's army will be the nucleus of the party and not vice versa"* (p. 116).

What are the implications of this? The most dramatic one, of course, is that it gives Castro an ideological principle which transcends any agreements he may have made with the Moscow-line communist parties. If guerrillas inevitably become the staunchest of Marxist-Leninist vanguards through their combat experience, why bother about so-called "orthodox" Marxist-Leninist parties already extant? And what is the only answer to the question of whom to support and strengthen, the guerrilla factions or the party? Debray asks the question and gives the answer: "The guerrilla force must be developed if the political vanguard is to be developed. That is why, at the present juncture, the principal stress must be laid on the development of guerrilla warfare and not on the strengthening of existing parties or the creation of new parties" (p. 116). How, then, could Castro "morally" do anything but actively support Bravo's group in Venezuela?

Debray and Muscovite Communism.

What made this ingenious bit of sophistry possible was not merely Debray's impressive mental agility; in a sense it is a logical consequence of several earlier Cuban feats of sleight-of-hand. The thesis that guerrillas inevitably become orthodox communists, for example, only became tenable after Moscow had tacitly acknowledged that the Cuban military was the predominant force in the Cuban Communist Party in late 1965. Debray's thesis, therefore, is the concluding jump in an almost circular game of semantic leapfrog. First Castro gained a foothold in the "socialist camp" by befriending the communists he had long held in contempt and by admitting them into his Cuban party (the ORI and later PURS). Once they had imparted a sufficient aura of orthodoxy to his party, he took away their influence and appropriated for himself their mantle of orthodoxy, the title of Communist. Once this had been accepted by Moscow, he could use this status to declare that all these other would-be Castro's in the hemisphere were at least as orthodox as he, and what could be more orthodox than that?

Debray is also very careful to disclaim all the familiar categories of "deviationism" into which Moscow might wish to relegate his doctrine. He specifically rejects Trotskyism as metaphysical and suicidal, and he specifically opposes Chinese-style political factionalism. What is needed, he says, is not new "political centers" of supposedly more orthodox Marxist-Leninist stripes—these fall into the same bureaucratic bog as the old parties: "The split among the Communist Parties, a corollary of international polemics, has occurred on the wrong issues,

. . . the true historic division between revolutionary Marxists on the one hand and the rest on the other is of another nature and operates on another terrain" (p. 123). In other words, revolutionaries must get off the "political" plane entirely and establish "military centers of insurrection," building upward from there. Debray is insistent that his doctrine is in no sense anticommunist. After all, Castro became "orthodox," and

> Whereas the ideology of the Cuban Rebel Army was not Marxist, the ideology of the new guerrilla commands is clearly so, just as the revolution which is their goal is clearly socialist and proletarian. It is precisely because their line is so clear and their determination so unalterable that they have had to separate themselves, at a certain point, from the existing vanguard parties and propose (as in Guatemala) or impose (as in Venezuela) their own political, ideological, and organizational ideas. . . . (pp. 106–107)

> Let it be noted that no part of the guerrilla movement has attempted to organize a new party. (p. 105)

The Debray doctrine is, in essence, a conscious Cuban attempt to subvert or displace existing communist parties and create effective guerrilla organizations which cannot be defined as competing "parties" or "factions." It is an ideological rationalization for the Tricontinent Conference and for the final abandonment of the 1964 Havana agreements, a rationalization which carefully leaves intact the one achievement which Moscow presumably considered most vital in these agreements—the Cuban split with Peking. It is a justification for as much direct Cuban aid to Latin American guerrillas as Castro sees fit to give, regardless of the nature of the government being attacked. Nowhere in Debray's theory is there a hint of Che Guevara's admission in *Guerrilla Warfare* that the insurrection must be delayed "until legal means of struggle are exhausted."

Notably absent in Debray's book is the role required of the communist countries, but Debray has alluded to this matter elsewhere. In an interview published in *Granma* in early February 1967, Debray gave the following summation of Cuba's contribution to Marxism-Leninism and international revolutionary experience:

1. The Cuban revolution introduced a new type of articulation, a new way of amalgamating political and military spheres in the movement's insurrectionary stage.
2. The Cuban revolution introduced a new articulation, a new amalgamation between the morale factor and the economic factor. For Cuba, morale is of great importance, a more important incentive than material stimulus in encouraging people to work and to produce material goods in the new society. Cuba, at the same time that it built a socialist society, established a moral communist foundation, including communist organizations.
3. A new type of unity or link between national and international spheres was introduced. In Cuba there is no alternative between building up socialism in one country and extending the revolution to many other countries. . . . This is a new articulation between the patriotic revolutionary and the international proletarian. One must admit that of all socialist countries, Cuba is the one that has advanced the most in this respect. This is because Cuba's interest is the interest of a cause and not only a state's interest. It is inconceivable that American revolution, or the revolution in any country in the underdeveloped world, can some day contradict the Cuban revolution's interests.

In conclusion, Debray brought up what is perhaps the most vital point—Castro's radical axis in the international communist movement: "One can use the same reasoning in Korea and Vietnam. This is why these three countries, Cuba, Vietnam and North Korea, and their three revolutions, have a close kinship, a friendship that is displayed before the world's eyes and has been endowed with the value of an important symbol."[5]

Almost all of the elements of Castro's stance are now present: the guerrilla doctrine which denies that communist parties are the revolutionary vanguard; the "moral incentives" doctrine favored by Che Guevara which denies Soviet economic theory of the last decade; the doctrine of placing aid to foreign revolutions above domestic prosperity thus denying the hoary Stalinist precept of "socialism in one country" and everything that has flowed from that precept; and finally, the open alignment with North Vietnam and North Korea, which implicitly denies Soviet leadership of the world communist movement. One element of Cuban thought not discussed by Debray is the concept of the coordinated "continental revolution" to counter the "global strategy of imperialism." This final doctrine, with its implicit denial that the U.S.S.R. is in fact coordinating international revolutionary action, is a recurring theme in speeches by Cubans and their current Latin American followers.

Moscow and the Traditional Parties

Soviet and traditional communist theory on Latin American revolution has never been willing to accept the idea that the *form* of struggle (armed versus unarmed, legal versus illegal) is a central strategic (as opposed to tactical) question. The questions of *alliances* and the positioning of the communists in "broad democratic and anti imperialist fronts" are the strategic questions; the form of struggle is a tactical matter, dependent on the attitudes of allies and the nature of the "oppression" practiced by the "ruling groups." According to the theory, if the alliances are properly forged and the resultant fronts strong enough, the result will be a government headed by the "national bourgeoisie" which will carry out an initial "bourgeois-democratic" revolution involving land reform, nationalization of heavy industry, confiscation of U.S. properties, and friendly relations with the U.S.S.R. In this phase, the influence of the local communists and the "socialist camp" will supposedly grow strong enough to become dominant on the national scene, thus allowing a gradual or sudden shift into the second, "socialist," stage of the revolution. Lacking such a growth of "progressive forces," a counterrevolution, as in Guatemala and Brazil, will reverse the gains made in the first revolution.

One of the most concise expositions of the Soviet theory in recent years is contained in the introduction to *The Liberation Movement in Latin America,* published in 1964 by the Soviet Academy of Science. The author of this article, S. S. Mikhailov, first describes in detail the class structure of Latin American society, the groups with which communists should seek alliances, the special role played by the "national bourgeoisie," and the ways in which communists must strengthen their position after the "bourgeois-democratic" revolution in order to thwart "counterrevolutionary" attempts. His verdict on forms of struggle is curt and to the point: Communists should prefer peaceful tactics but should master all forms of struggle to take advantage of any contingency; armed struggle cannot be launched until there is an "immediate revolutionary situation"; exclusive emphasis on armed struggle—growing out of an attempt at "mechanical" application of the Cuban experience elsewhere in the hemisphere—can only result in depriving the "revolutionary arsenal" of other vital weapons, separation of the "vanguard" from the masses, and conceivably the annihilation of that vanguard.[6]

More recent Soviet pronouncements have added only minor modifications and elaborations to this analysis. The articles in *Kommunist* later in 1964 (see pp. 24–25) give relatively greater stress to the peasantry as the chief ally of the communists, but still insist on the leading role of the "working class." Soviet writings of 1965, working on the popular front theme and the Dominican example, stress the importance of seeking allies within the national armed forces and even within the political groups in power. The struggle for seemingly nonrevolutionary goals, went the theory, would create broad alliances which would inevitably *become* revolutionary when faced with repressions from "the domestic oligarchy and U.S. imperialism." Perhaps the most authoritative Soviet statement of this period appeared in the September 1965 *Kommunist*:

Here, in the course of daily struggle for economic demands, during political demonstrations and strikes, if in the very midst of pre-elections campaigns, broad democratic coalitions are being formed around the working class and its organizations. The working class, the urban middle strata, and the peasantry are being rallied to them gradually, and it is exactly these coalitions which are capable of heading the revolutionary process, of bringing about radical anti-imperialistic and social changes.[7]

It was almost immediately after this definitive statement of the popular front doctrine that the whole traditional communist approach began to be undermined by a series of Castroite moves. In quick succession, Castro defined his guerrilla army as an orthodox communist party, Ojeda and Bravo set up their "unified politico-military command," and the Tricontinent Conference glorified guerrillas and set the stage for Debray's thesis.

This resurgent Castroism was by no means an insignificant threat to Soviet doctrine. One of the central arguments in the Soviet dispute with the Chinese was over the role of the party in the first stages of the revolution. Maoist theory insisted that the party had to gain the leading role at this point; the Soviets denied that it was always necessary or possible. The Cubans agreed with the Soviets on this question in order to postulate with increasing adamance that some force other than the party— namely the guerrilla nucleus—*had* to take the leadership at this point. The same theoretical loophole which allowed Moscow to tell Arab communists that Nasser and Ben Bella were thoroughly progressive "revolutionary democrats" also enabled Castro to tell Latin American communists that their leadership wasn't necessary.

It was not surprising, therefore, that signs of a tightening of this loophole began to appear in late 1966. A September 7, 1966 article in *Pravda* by Yuri Arbatov, for example, contained the following admonition:

   . . . for the socialist revolution . . . a socialist consciousness is required which, as V. I. Lenin pointed out, *does not arise spontaneously* and which must be carried into the movement of the workers class from outside by its conscious vanguard—the revolutionary Marxist party.

This is all the more valid for a revolutionary movement in which the non-proletarian masses play the chief role. National liberation and democratic revolutions can be victorious without a socialist consciousness. But only the latter's introduction into the national liberation and democratic movement can open the path for the transition to the higher, socialist stage of the revolution.[8]

This was surely meant to be read in the same context as the statement of the Venezuelan communist newspaper two weeks later:

> No one could overlook the fact that it was, to a great extent, the support of the Cuban Communists to Fidel Castro and the left wing of the "26 July" movement which enabled the revolution to advance, to get support from the rebel army and the masses, at home, and from the socialist world, abroad, in order to defeat the counterrevolution . . . and bring about qualitative change in the national democratic revolution, which was converted into the socialist revolution.[9]

In March 1967, not long after Debray's book had made its contribution to communist debate, an article in *Pravda* gave a more explicit and authoritative statement of the importance of communist parties:

> The Communists justly maintain that with the intensification of the attacks of U.S. imperialism on the honor and sovereignty of the Latin American peoples, any underestimation of the role of the Marxist-Leninist party of the working class in the national liberation struggle, any weakening of the Communist parties and, even more, any splitting of their ranks, whatever motives may lie behind it, would bring irremediable damage to the vital interests of their countries and peoples.[10]

In addition to this reassertion of the party role, the Soviets continued to avoid any application of the term "revolutionary democratic" to movements in Latin America other than Castro's Twenty-sixth of July Movement.

Party supremacy was not the only question on which Soviet theory had been challenged. There was still the perennial debate over "forms of struggle." Here, as we have noted in regard to Venezuela, the Soviets generally avoided confronting the issue but still clearly intimated their inclination toward legal tactics in most cases. Increasingly, however, they seemed to be drawn toward the compromise formula of "all forms of struggle at once," a formula apparently first seized upon by the Colombian Communist Party in a desperate attempt to stay on top of the diverse forces at work in the Colombian left. A September 1966 article in *Izvestia*, for example, first spoke approvingly of partisan warfare in Colombia and urged against underestimating the role of the peasantry. The author concluded, however, with the observation that "the armed path not only does not exclude but makes the use of other forms of struggle obligatory in the same nations."[11]

The "all forms of struggle" formula did not appear likely to become a permanent feature of pro-Soviet communist theory in the hemisphere, however. The traditional communist doctrine of being *prepared* for all forms of struggle was one thing; using them all at once was patent nonsense. The party leaders in Latin America certainly knew this, and the Cubans were not likely to encourage Castroites to rally around this slogan. Debray's book refers derisively to "happy pragmatists who would like to see all forms of struggle used together, and to see how they would all work out together."[12]

Finally, the Soviets faced the new Cuban doctrine of internationalism, which asserted that socialist countries should not proceed with building communist abundance until the world-wide defeat of "imperialism" has been accomplished. Of all the Cuban "contributions to Marxism-Leninism" this struck the most sensitive nerve: "The building of communism in the U.S.S.R. and the comprehensive perfection of the Soviet socialist society are the basic contribution of our party and of the entire Soviet people to the world revolutionary process," stated Yuri Arbatov in *Pravda*. This assertion came exactly one week after Castro had declared that the Cubans would "never desire the attainment of their future at the unworthy price of betraying their international duties." Arbatov's article added, for anyone who missed the point, that construction of communism in the U.S.S.R. "is also regarded as the main international duty of the Soviet people by the fraternal Communist and workers parties."

Arbatov's subsequent analysis provides revealing insight into the thinking of at least some of the Soviet leaders on the question of aid to national liberation movements. Arbatov first denies that any doctrine precludes giving material aid to foreign revolutions, but then he refers to the "dialectical aspect" of the question:

The resolution of many economic problems now facing our country requires a further increase in the well-being and culture of the working people, an increase in the material and cultural benefits offered to them by the society. Naturally, it is possible, based on the revolutionary enthusiasm and high consciousness of the people and on their international-

140

COMPETING REVOLUTIONARY DOCTRINES

ism, to conduct matters in the course of a relatively brief historical period so as not to raise the living standard but at the same time to engage in successful economic construction. But no kind of high consciousness permits the transformation of such a situation into a permanent state. The economic laws will inevitably prove to be stronger; they will begin to take revenge, they will revenge themselves in a thousand ways, and in the end there will be a drop in labor productivity and a slowing down of economic development.

Not only positive examples of the socialist countries have their influence on the revolutionary processes proceeding in the world, but also failures, difficulties, and errors.

Finally, Arbatov answers Castro directly:

Sometimes even today one happens to hear doubts: is it possible to build a communist society if imperialism still remains on our planet? The problem should be presented the other way around—can imperialism hold on long if a communist society opposes it on part of the planet?[13]

Different shading and nuances of meaning in Soviet theoretical statements in these areas could be cited at some length. There is ample reason for believing that Soviet leaders are not and have never been unanimous in their views on such recent theoretical innovations as the "revolutionary democratic" trends and such perennial issues as the precise role to be played by the party at each stage in the revolution.[14] Nonetheless the FALN-Castro-Debray challenge to traditional communist theory on questions of Latin American revolution has been met with a fairly consistent pattern: 1) the importance of the party has been reasserted; 2) the emphasis on "broad democratic and anti-imperialist fronts" has been maintained, with some hedging in the direction of endorsing "all forms of struggle";

3) the idea of increasing aid to liberation movements at the expense of any significant deterrent to Soviet economic growth has been forcefully rejected; and 4) the idea of international coordination of liberation struggles via the tricontinent organization or any similar structure has been pointedly ignored and implicitly rejected in Soviet reassertions of the right of each party to set its own line.

Motivations of the Divergent Doctrines

Moscow. Of the major protagonists, the Soviets were the most consistent and most readily explainable in their behavior. The Soviet Union is unique in the modern world in having a leading role in each of two dramatically opposed cultures and value systems: the international underground of communism and revolution, and the "respectable" international community of great powers, nuclear powers, well-to-do northern powers. Not since the Cuban missile crisis have the Soviets entertained any immediate hopes of adding another Latin American nation to the "socialist camp," but their need to enhance (or even maintain) their leading role in the international revolutionary culture has kept them playing the revolutionary game in Latin America, as elsewhere. In both the "revolutionary" and the "respectable" games, the Soviets have behaved with the purest of pragmatism, but a pragmatism beset by the problem that a gain in one game almost invariably means a loss in the other.

It is the role of Soviet theoreticians somehow to alter this equation, to introduce double-talk and pseudorevolution or pseudorespectability so that gains in one culture can be ignored or even claimed as gains in the other. In Latin America, the theoreticians' dilemma becomes particularly difficult. Unlike Africa or the Middle East, Latin America offers no radical nationalist governments which can be defined as "revolutionary" by means of such formulas as "revolutionary democratic." And it offers no areas where communist parties are so sparse or weak that Moscow can define its state to state ties as fulfilling the function of an absent proletarian vanguard.* Finally, there is always Cuba, a constant reminder that Latin American revolution cannot be written off as hopeless under the old shibboleth of geographical fatalism. Castro's presence in the Carribbean also presents a constant challenge to any attempts to define revolution away into the distant future.

Nonetheless, the Soviet theoreticians made a valiant attempt, largely because conditions in early 1965 seemed particularly propitious. Through a remarkably successful maneuver in the revolutionary game (the 1964 Havana Conference), the Soviets seemed to be in a particularly strong position in Latin America. The Dominican revolt had shown the "revolutionary" potential of the "bourgeois nationalists" and the resultant hemispheric crisis seemed to brighten dramatically the prospects for success

---

* There has been, however, one intriguing indication that Soviet theoreticians might try this tack. One writer lumped Latin America together with Africa and Asia as an area where "the national proletariat is rather weak," where "the great mass of the population is composed of the peasantry," and where "a socialist consciousness of the population could be achieved primarily only with the assistance of the international proletariat" (G. Kim and P. Shastitko, in *Pravda*, September 14, 1966).

in the "respectable" game. A resurrection of the popular front theme seemed just the ticket for holding onto gains in the "revolutionary" game while advancing Soviet great-power goals through state-to-state relations with the Latin American democratic reformers whom the popular front doctrine made respectable.

President Leoni in Venezuela was just such a reformist democrat. He had opposed U.S. action in the Dominican Republic; he had plenty of possible areas of friction with the U.S., and he or members of his party showed signs of being willing to talk about such things as a return to legality by Venezuelan communists and the expansion of relations with the U.S.S.R. The change in Soviet perspective regarding Venezuela was unmistakable. In the 1965 edition of the authoritative *Great Soviet Encyclopedia*, Leoni was described entirely in negative terms: He was seen as following a "pro-U.S. orientation," "hostile" towards Cuba. In the 1966 edition he was described in neutral or positive terms: He was opposed to "unilateral U.S. intervention in Latin America," unwilling to participate in the Second Rio Conference, opposed to an "Inter-American Peace Force" in the OAS.[15]

The major remaining obstacle to an expansion of Venezuelan ties with Moscow was the Venezuelan guerrilla war. The popular front doctrine, of course, provided for this, too. The only problem was that the guerrillas wouldn't buy it, Castro wouldn't buy it, and the Soviets, unable to let well enough alone, were still trying for additional gains in the "revolutionary" game of the Tricontinent Conference.

Cuba. Why was Castro unwilling to accept the double Soviet game in Latin America? Surely by

1965 he could see that his own experience had been unique, that his own strategy for victory was the one the U.S. and the Latin American governments were best geared up to foil, that his identification with international communism effectively prevented any "guerrilla nucleus" elsewhere in the hemisphere from gathering about it a broad array of noncommunist supporters such as he had gained in his final drive to victory in Cuba. Surely Castro could see that the only real prospect of communists coming to power in another Latin American country was in the event of a sharp political crisis, a breakdown of governmental authority. And in such a situation wasn't the insidious opportunism of traditional communists likely to be more effective than Castroite partisan warfare which placed all the forces of anti-communism and of order on their guard? Finally, didn't the economic benefits of a turn toward respectability far outweigh anything he could gain from support of a few losing guerrilla struggles in Latin America? Couldn't he see the advantages of applying here the same pragmatism he used in economic dealings with Europe—that by doing so he could gradually wear away his economic and political isolation in Latin America, while sowing seeds of discord between the U.S. and anyone who would deal with him?

The answer may well be that he saw these possibilities and rejected them. More noteworthy even than the fact that he rejected them, however, was the way in which he rejected them. This was not a carefully planned, pragmatically calculated reassertion of Castroism. Initially, Castro probably did accept much of the Soviet design; his rapprochement with the Soviets in 1965 seemed genuine. Guevara's departure was an indisputable fact, as was the political eclipse of his former protégés in the Cuban government. Castro's statements on communist unity in his March 13, 1965 speech committed him to a stance he would never have taken if he had not then been convinced of the propriety of the November 1964 Havana agreements. Castro may not have been ideologically comfortable in the Soviet camp at this point, but he had evidently become resigned to accepting his role and making the best of it.

Castro's ultimate rejection of the Soviet design was not so much the result of its objective failure (although it certainly did fail) as it was his own belated recognition of the full implications of the Soviet design and his sudden realization that there might be an alternative. His rejection of the Soviet design developed spasmodically, and, until late 1966, mostly as a reaction to specific pressures or revelations. In the uproar of the Tricontinent Conference, Castro was almost certainly playing things by ear, and several of his other more dramatic actions bore the earmarks of heat-of-the-moment decision making. The net effect of these decisions, however, was a progressively firmer and more adamant rejection of Moscow's line.

Foremost among the factors pushing Castro toward at least a verbal repudiation of Soviet doctrine were the attacks on Castro's revolutionary integrity from Latin American revolutionary leftists following the 1964 Havana conference, after the Dominican crisis, and in the period surrounding the Tricontinent Conference. Castro's sensitivity to such criticism was not merely the reaction of an exceedingly proud and vain individual; it was the reaction of a leader whose most crucial base of support had been threatened. Castro has consciously resisted resting his preeminence in Cuba on an institutional structure which would make his unique personality traits irrelevant. This strategy has undoubtedly reflected a realization that to do so would make him replaceable and tempt the Soviets or others to conspire for his early retirement. In any case, Castro has behaved as if his very survival depended on maintaining his charismatic qualities as the Cuban "Líder Máximo" and on sustaining his heroic myth of revolutionary fidelity.

At times it has seemed conceivable that Castro's need for a heroic myth might be redirected inward, that he might be satisfied in a role as the great economic genius of Cuba, as the agrarian reformer *par excellence* and the builder of Cuban socialism. This apparently is what the Soviets were banking on in 1965 (the Cuban "year of agriculture"). But the rewards of this role were pallid, slow in appearing, and they offered nothing to Castro's foreign constituency. Castro, after all, had always seen himself as more than just a Cuban leader—he was a 'second Bolivar,' a 'continental liberator.' His legend depended on his messianic persistence in leading insurrection when virtually all others, including the communists, had written his chances off as negligible. His legend also involved internationalism; he had not won with Cuban arms and funds alone. To have it now asserted that he was an accomplice in denying aid to other heroic groups who were just where he had been ten years earlier was an intolerable challenge to the very source of his claimed legitimacy.

A second factor was Castro's total lack of identification with the traditional Latin American communist leaders. When placed in a situation where his image was at stake in any way, Castro could not bring himself to side with the stodgy, aging, self-disciplined communist party functionaries and against the brash young Fidelistas. Castro's obvious preference for youth and heroism above painstaking caution and organization was even formalized in Debray's book as the "profound link between biology and ideology" wherever armed struggle is in progress (p. 102). Indeed, a good case can be made for the thesis that Castro persisted in rejecting the Soviet doctrine in part because he was not really interested in *communist* victory per se. A communist takeover via popular front tactics and a bloodless coup d'etat would not be true "revolution." There would be none of the guerrillas who according to Debray have the best training to become socialist officials; there would only be the "bureaucrats" that Castro has felt obliged to weed out of his party to make way for the truer vanguard of Twenty-sixth of July graduates. And of course a *via pacifica* victory would offer no confirmation that Castro had showed the world the unique Latin American way of revolution.

One of the more pragmatic reasons for Castro's insistence on guerrilla warfare is his unquestionable desire to sabotage any reformist solutions to Latin America's problems. The vehemence of Castro's attacks on Presidents Frei and Leoni—and on reformists in general—leaves no doubt that he considers successful reformism to be a much graver threat to his objectives in Latin America than the continued survival of unpopular dictatorships. It is here, perhaps, that the divergence of Soviet and

Cuban viewpoints is at its greatest. To the Soviets, reformism of the sort practiced by Frei or Leoni is basically to the good; it is usually accompanied by expanded relations with the U.S.S.R., greater freedom for domestic communists (of the legalist, pro-Moscow stripe), increased independence from the U.S., and frictions with conservative forces of the hemisphere which can handily be described as an "aggravation of contradictions." To Castro, however, such reformism is a frontal challenge to his claim that the excesses of his revolution were a historical necessity. Likewise, if the intermediate "national democratic" stage in the two-stage revolution of Soviet doctrine were to be achieved as a result of popular front tactics, it might well last long enough to seriously discredit the course of Castro's headlong rush into a communist dictatorship.

An even more pragmatic aspect of Cuban doctrine concerns the relationship of foreign "liberation wars" to the security of Cuba itself. It is not entirely chest-beating when Castro or Debray asserts a unique "unity of interests" between the Cuban revolution and revolutions elsewhere in the third world. When Castro says that the best form of solidarity with Vietnam is the intensification of revolutionary struggles elsewhere, he is placing himself in Vietnamese shoes. There are innumerable signs that Castro lives in definite fear of the day when the U.S. and the U.S.S.R. are not committed to at least indirect confrontation over some liberation war. The U.S. and OAS, he reasons, if they were not otherwise militarily committed, might well try to expend greater efforts to "get rid of Castro." Or the U.S.S.R. and the U.S. might, in an atmosphere of detente, come to some general East-West settlement which would leave him out in the cold.

Finally—and this constitutes a bogey in its own right—a general decline in Latin American guerrilla struggles might lead to expansion of Soviet interests in the rest of Latin America outweighing their stake in Cuba. Castro's anger was genuine when in his March 13, 1967 speech he referred caustically to AP reports that the Soviets might prefer entry into Latin America via an embassy in Caracas to a "blind alley" in Havana. He reminded Moscow that the Colombian government "did not hesitate" to arrest the Secretary-General of the Colombian Communist Party at the same time that a Soviet delegation was in the country to negotiate economic and cultural agreements. Then he returned to his bitterness over Venezuela:

> Such is the friendly spirit of those oligarchs. . . . Cannot perhaps proof of the lack of independence and of the hypo-critical international policy of those puppet governments be seen from the way those in Venezuela speak, trying to de-mand that the UAR quit the tricontinental organization and that the USSR practically sever its relations with Cuba, the "blind alley," and enter the wide, wide open and friendly door offered it by the Venezuelan Government—the govern-ment that has murdered the most communists in this con-tinent?
>
> No matter what the others do, we Marxist-Leninists will never re-establish relations with such governments.
>
> What would the Vietnamese revolutionaries think if we sent delegations to South Vietnam to negotiate with the puppet government in Saigon?

It seems entirely plausible that the note of urgency in Cuban insistence on "proletarian international-ism" and coordinated "continental revolution" stem directly from a belief that only these few languishing guerrilla struggles in Venezuela and Colombia stand in the way of broadened governmental ties with the U.S.S.R. which might very well make Castro's regime look like a "blind alley."

The final element in Castro's rejection of Soviet designs was, of course, his growing awareness of the alternatives. The experience of the Tricontinent Conference revealed to him that his split with Peking did not place him inexorably under Soviet discipline. It showed him that there was a viable third position and it convinced him that the only way he could prevent Moscow's "respectable" international game from pushing him further and further aside was to play the "revolutionary" international game with a vengeance. The events of this period also showed Castro that there were two other members of the communist camp, North Korea and North Vietnam, who shared his vital interest in manipulating the "revolutionary" game to thwart Soviet inclinations toward respectability and compromise.

The key element in this strategy was the tricontinent organization, AALAPSO, which provided a structure for playing the "revolutionary" game along rules not set by Moscow but which Moscow could not disavow. Here at last was an organizational vehicle for Castroism. No longer could Castro's commitment to "unity," "solidarity," and co-ordination of strategies lead him inexorably into agreements such as that of Havana in 1964. "Let them call us heretics," Castro was finally able to say on August 29, 1966, "Who cares?" After all, "This Cuban attitude, this attitude which our people have won by their dignity and their struggle, is recognized by the revolutionary movements, and it is recognized by the nations. This authority and prestige of the Cuban revolution was demonstrated at the Tricontinental Conference. It was demonstrated at the Latin American Students Conference. It has been in evidence at every opportunity and in every international event." Castro, there could be no doubt, had learned the arts of international communist gamesmanship. He had graduated from disorganized adolescent rebellion into deep involvement in his own brand of "new politics."

Toward the Future

Since mid-1967, events have added to the picture but not altered its basic outlines, which achieved their fullest expression in Castro's March 13, 1967 speech. The inconclusive confrontation between Castroites and traditional communists at the July 1967 Latin American Solidarity Conference was a predictable consequence of the Soviet-Cuban stalemate developed over the preceding two years. Castro had every reason to build up the Latin American Solidarity Organization as another trump in the international revolutionary game, but he could ill afford to push his pet themes to the point of compelling Moscow to repudiate the organization. Hence, it was to his advantage to keep some of the pro-Moscow communists of the hemisphere within LASO, preferably as a weak and ineffectual minority.

In the field of revolutionary actions, attention focused briefly on Bolivia, where both Guevara and Debray turned up, pursuing or observing their theories in practice. Guevara's failure was a blow to Castro's doctrines, but could be readily passed off as a consequence of Guevara's personal impetuousness. Che had long since ceased to be indispensable to Castro, and the Bolivian venture had never taken on the vital personal importance to Fidel of the Venezuelan guerrilla movement. Its collapse did nothing to alter the pattern of forces which had drawn him into his renewed efforts to foment Latin American revolution in the Castroite mold. Cuban propaganda continued to focus on Venezuela, though here Havana had to deal with a situation in which neither Bravo nor any other leader was successfully asserting firm "politico-military" direction of the guerrilla efforts.

Finally, in Cuba itself, the revelations concerning the "Escalante micro-faction" in January 1968 brought still more dirty linen to light. There had been, it turned out, pro-Soviet Cubans in Havana critical of Castro's rebellious stance toward Moscow during 1966 and 1967. And by covertly lobbying (or conspiring) on behalf of Moscow, the PCV, and general communist orthodoxy, they undoubtedly contributed to the exacerbation of Cuban-Soviet and Cuban-PCV differences.

Moscow through all this remained outwardly impassive, and the terms of the game seemed likely to reinforce this stance. Nowhere on the scene was there the key ingredient which had brought about the Soviet reinvolvement in 1964: a major potential gain in the Sino-Soviet battle for world revolutionary leadership. To buy Castro off would now be virtually impossible. Even if it could be done again after the experience of the 1964 Havana conference, it would give Moscow at best a temporary respite at an exorbitant cost. A repeat of the 1964 conference, for example, would undoubtedly commit the Soviets once more to a militant line running directly counter to their efforts to cultivate state-to-state relations in the hemisphere. On the other hand, an attempt to discipline the Cuban leader would risk causing severe havoc in Soviet relations with North Korea and North Vietnam, not to mention threatening the survival of communism in Cuba itself. And in the long run, the costs of any sanction against Castro would find their way back into the Soviet subsidy of his regime.

Thus the prospects remain in favor of an indefinite continuation of the Soviet-Cuban divergence over Latin American revolutionary strategy. Any early repetition of the joint commitment to support an insurgency such as the FALN guerrilla war at more than token levels seems unlikely. Both powers are focusing on something less than victory in the Latin American revolutionary movement, if for opposite reasons. The Soviet reasons incline them toward caution even where slim chances for revolutionary success might exist; Cuba's reasons produce an inclination to keep insurgencies going now, even if the longer run chances for revolution are thereby jeopardized. It is not insignificant that the Cuban slogan of "additional Vietnams" in Latin America has gradually taken precedence over the call for "more Cubas." The implication of "new Cubas" was new revolutionary victories; the implication of "more Vietnams" is more conflagrations to over-extend the U.S. and keep Moscow committed to the revolutionary game. Moscow needs its Latin American communists—however far from power they may be—to maintain the "world movement" and to keep some control over the terms of the revolutionary games it must play. Castro needs his own international following who will kindle revolutionary fires for their own sake in order to maintain his revolutionary image and his independence from Moscow. New radical-leftist revolutions may still succeed in Latin America, but they will have neither Moscow nor Havana to thank for their success.

NOTE: Unless otherwise noted, the source for quotations from Fidel Castro's speeches is Radio Havana for the day following the indicated speech date.

Chapter II.

1. Although concrete proof of regular Soviet funding is sparse, the relative affluence of Latin American CP's as compared to other parties of similar size is convincing circumstantial evidence of outside finances. Statements by former communists also confirm the general picture of regular but fairly small-scale Soviet subsidies of every Moscow-line communist party. See Rollie E. Poppino, *International Communism in Latin America* (New York: Macmillan, 1964), pp. 154–171.

2. See, for example, J. Posadas, "The Expulsion of Guevara from Cuba is a Blow to the Development of the Cuban Socialist Revolution," *Voz Proletaria* (Buenos Aires), October 27, 1965, pp. 3ff. Posadas and others of his stripe have not claimed that Guevara was a Trotskyite, but they have said that he was moving toward the Trotskyite position at the time of his disappearance.

3. One Soviet writer, for example, stated in July 1962 that "Actual experience and the practice of the national liberation movement has proved the untenability of the theory of non-violence." A. Kurtsev, *International Affairs*, No. 7 (July 1962), pp. 94ff.

4. Anonymous, "Revolutionary Studies—The Great Truths of the Third Congress," *¿Qué?* (Caracas), No. 112 (September 9, 1966), p. 12.

5. *World Marxist Review*, October 1964, p. 41. (Hereinafter cited as *WMR*.)

6. See Ernst Halperin, "Latin America," *Survey*, January 1965, p. 164.

7. *Hoy* (Havana), March 9, 1963, quoted in Theodore Draper, *Castroism: Theory and Practice* (New York: Praeger, 1965) p. 42.

8. "Declaration conjunta sovietico-cubana," *Cuba Socialista,* June 1963, pp. 17–18.

9. The Chinese had stated that the Chilean *via pacifica*

"stands in sharp contrast to the revolutionary way of Fidel Castro." Luis Corvalan, "The Peaceful Way—A Form of Revolution," *WMR*, December 1963, p. 8.
10. Castro's speech of September 10, 1964, quoted in *Obra Revolucionaria*, No. 20 (1964), p. 24.

Chapter III.

1. Herbert S. Dinerstein, *Soviet Policy in Latin America*, Rand Corporation, Memorandum RM-4967-PR, May 1966, pp. 28–30.
2. A. Sivolobov, "Krestianskoe Dvizhenie v Latinskoi Amerike," *Kommunist*, No. 12 (August 1964), pp. 100–107.
3. Palmiro Togliatti, "On International Working Class Unity," *Political Affairs*, October 1964, pp. 38–40, translated from the Italian CP journal *Renascita*, September 5, 1964.
4. *Pravda*, October 17, 1964, p. 3. The text of Togliatti's memorandum had been published in *Pravda* (September 10, 1964) before Khrushchev's ouster.
5. In preparation for the January 1966 Havana Tricontinent Conference, the Cubans endorsed the FAR, rather than the Thirteenth of November Revolutionary Movement led by Yon Sosa.
6. Martin Balanta, "Rupture between Castro and Peiping," *Segunda República* (La Paz), January 30, 1966, p. 4.

Chapter IV.

1. Guevara was in Peking February 3–9, 1965. New China News Agency, February 9, 1965.
2. On February 24, at the Afro-Asian Economic Seminar in Algiers, for example, Guevara suggested openly that the socialist countries were adopting capitalist policies in their commercial relationships with underdeveloped countries.
3. See Adolfo Gilly's article "A Conference Without Glory and Without Program," *Monthly Review*, April 1966, pp. 27–29. Gilly and others also allege that Guevara's last known appearance was before a group of Cuban Trotskyites and imply that Guevara's association with them in opposition to Castro resulted in his "liquidation."
4. V. Listov, "Big Stick Against a Small Nation," *New Times*, No. 20 (May 17, 1965), p. 11.
5. The timing of the conferences two months after the logical date for anniversary celebrations (the Seventh Congress was in July–August 1935) suggests that the potential of the Seventh Comintern Congress theme was only belatedly recognized,

perhaps only after Soviet leaders had evaluated the success of midsummer trial balloons.

6. B. T. Rudenko, "The Ideas of the Seventh Comintern Congress and the Anti-imperialist Movements in Latin America," in a compilation of the October 1965 Moscow conference documents entitled *Za yedinstvo vsekh revolyutsionnykh i demokraticheskikh sil,* Moscow: Nauk, 1966, translated in *Joint Publications Research Service,* 36, 691, July 26, 1966, pp. 88–92. (Hereinafter cited as JPRS.)

Chapter V.

1. From Branco Lazitch, "The Venezuelan Communist Party and the Sino-Soviet Conflict," *Est et Ouest* (Paris), No. 335 (February 1–15, 1965), p. 2.

2. For example, in June 1965, the Italian Communist Party and assorted international communist front organizations organized an "International Conference for an Amnesty of Political Prisoners in Venezuela" in Italy. An article in the June 1965 *WMR*, pp. 86–88, "For Amnesty in Venezuela," was typical of the advance publicity for the conference.

3. *Pravda*, April 4 and June 26, 1964, and July 17, 1964, p. 5, and July 18, 1964, p. 1.

4. Carlos Lopez, "The Communist Party of Venezuela and the Present Situation," *WMR*, October 1964, pp. 18–25.

5. Djuka Julius, *Politika* (Belgrade), October 9, 1964.

6. Radio Moscow, September 19, 1964.

7. Communiqué of the Havana conference, *Pravda*, January 19, 1965, p. 3.

8. Interview of Eduardo Gallegos Mancera in *Pravda*, September 26, 1964, p. 3.

9. "Outline for the Report of the Resolutions of the Seventh Plenum of the Central Committee of the Venezuelan Communist Party," *Confidencial* (news service publication of the Venezuelan Ministry of Interior Relations), No. 26 (July 29, 1965), pp. 9–10, translated in U.S. Department of Commerce, *JPRS*, 10,564, 1965, pp. 56–57. (Hereinafter cited as "Seventh Plenum Outline.")

10. Interview of Douglas Bravo in *Sucesos para Todos* (Mexico), quoted by Radio Havana, December 24, 1966.

11. *La República* (Caracas), March 25, 1965.

12. "Seventh Plenum Outline," pp. 57, 63.

13. Castro's speech of March 13, 1967, Havana domestic radio, March 14, 1967.

14. "Resolutions of the Seventh Plenum of the Central Com-

mittee of the PCV," *Confidencial*, No. 24 (June 30, 1965),
p. 2, translated in *JPRS*, 10,564, 1965, pp. 39–40.
15. *El Siglo* (Santiago), October 14, 1965.
16. See *Pravda*, July 3, 1965, p. 3.
17. Lionel Soto's speech, quoted in *El Siglo* (Santiago), October 18, 1965.
18. See *Pravda*, October 12, 1965 for partial listing, and *El Siglo* (Chile), October 7–18, 1965.
19. *El Nacional* (Caracas), August 29, 1965.
20. Quoted from the September 1965 PCV declaration in "Discord Between the Communist Party and the Revolutionary Leftist Movement in Venezuela," *Est et Ouest* (Paris), No. 354 (January 1–15), 1966. (Hereinafter cited as "Discord, PCV-MIR.")
21. Douglas Bravo interview, *Sucesos para Todos* (Mexico), December 24, 1966, quoted by Radio Havana, December 24, 1966.
22. Quoted in "Discord, PCV-MIR, *Est et Ouest* (Paris).
23. Castro's speech of March 13, 1967, Radio Havana, March 14, 1967.
24. Quoted in "Discord, PCV-MIR," *Est et Ouest* (Paris).
25. Quoted in Castro's speech of March 13, 1967, Radio Havana, March 14, 1967.
26. Castro, *ibid.*
27. *New York Times*, October 17, 1965.
28. Interview of Douglas Bravo in *Sucesos*, December 24, 1967.
29. Fabricio Ojeda's letter of June 4, 1966 to Castro as quoted in Castro's March 13, 1967 speech, Radio Havana, March 14, 1967.
30. Castro's speech of October 3, 1965, Radio Havana, October 4, 1965.
31. Castro's speech of September 28, 1965, Radio Havana, September 29, 1965.

Chapter VI.

1. The matter was raised at the AAPSO Council Meeting in Bandung, April 1961. See Council of the OAS *Report on the First Afro-Asian-Latin American Peoples Solidarity Conference and its Projections* (Washington, D.C.: Pan American Union, November 28, 1966), Vol. I, pp. 10–11. (Hereinafter cited as Council of the OAS *Report*.)
2. *Ibid.*, Vol. I, pp. 14–15.

3. See for example *Pravda*, November 15, 1965.

4. Council of the OAS *Report*, Vol. I, p. 16.

5. *Ibid.*, p. 18.

6. Castro's speech of January 2, 1966, Radio Havana, January 2, 1966.

7. Full text of speech in Council of the OAS *Report*, Vol. II, pp. 41–45.

8. Council of the OAS *Report*, Vol. I, pp. 42–43.

9. *New China News Agency*, International service, January 19, 1966.

10. Ch'en Lo-min, "The Struggle of the Asian, African, and Latin American People's Solidarity Conference," *Shih-chieh Chih-shih* (Peking), February 10, 1966, pp. 15–18, translated in *JPRS*, 10,010.

11. Radio Havana, January 3, 1966.

12. Text of speech translated from *Cuba Socialista* in Council of the OAS *Report*, Vol. II, pp. 47–63.

13. Giuseppi dall'Ongaro, "Castro's Four Delusions," *Il Giornale d'Italia* (Rome), January 22–23, 1966, p. 3, translated in *JPRS*, 34,172, 1966.

14. Resolution on the Training of National Cadres, Resolution of the Economic Committee and General Declaration, Council of the OAS *Report*, Vol II, pp. 133, 157, 181 (emphasis supplied).

15. Belgrade domestic radio, January 4, 1966.

16. Council of the OAS *Report*, Vol. II, p. 253.

17. *Partisans* (Paris), February-March, 1966, pp. 106–7.

18. For example, according to a June 14, 1966 report by the Cuban news agency *Prensa Latina*, the Cuban delegate to the Sofia Assembly of the World Federation of Democratic Youth made a lengthy speech accusing the organization of lack of support for revolutionary movements, insufficient attention to Latin America, softness towards Western-oriented youth groups, and "interminable discussions" with "sterile results."

19. Council of the OAS *Report*, Vol. I. pp. 78–82.

20. Castro in interview with *Al Ahram*, January 29, 1966.

21. Quoted in "Reply of the Government of Uruguay to the Soviet Note on the Tricontinental Conference and Summary of the Text of the Russian Note," Council of the OAS *Report*, Vol. II, pp. 285–88.

22. U.N. Document S/7134, February 11, 1966, text in Council of the OAS *Report*, Vol. II, pp. 291–94.

23. *Pravda*, February 2, 1966.

24. Radio Havana, October 26, 1966.

NOTES

Chapter VII.

1. *Le República* (Caracas), February 25, 1966.
2. See *Juventud Rebelde* (Havana), March 15, 1966, p. 2, and *Granma*, February 15–20, 1966.
3. *Pravda*, April 2, 1966, p. 7.
4. "Internal Bulletin of the PCV Concerning Sanctions against Douglas Bravo," May 18, 1966, one of a series of communist documents published by the Venezuelan periodical *Confidencial*, No. 32 (August 1966), pp. 1–55, translated in *JPRS*, 38,275, October 21, 1966, pp. 13–16. (Hereinafter cited as May 18 "Internal Bulletin" of PCV.)
5. See proposal by Deputy Jesus Filardo Rodriguez, *El Nacional* (Caracas), February 13, 1966.
6. Interview of Elias Manuit on Radio Havana, November 19, 1966.
7. The minutes of the April 22 meeting were signed by Ojeda, Bravo, Elias Manuit, Lunar Marquez, and Pedro Vargas Castejon. Both documents are included in *Confidencial*, No. 32 (August 1966), translated in *JPRS,* 38,275, pp. 5–7.
8. The MIR reply, undated, appears in *Ibid.*, pp. 25–26. Ojeda's acceptance of the MIR's conditions dated June 2, appears in *Ibid.*, pp. 40–42; Américo Martin was not identified as the Secretary-General candidate in either letter, but signed as such in the May 30 letter to Castro which appeared in *Granma*.
9. May 18 "Internal Bulletin" of PCV, pp. 14–15.
10. *Confidencial*, No. 32, pp. 19–20.
11. *Ibid.*, p. 45. Except for the section concerning Ojeda's request for Cuban funds, Castro's version of the letter was almost identical to the *Confidencial* version. The one other discrepancy is the phrase "That is, financially throttled the guerrilla centers. . . ." This appears to be Castro's own embellishment.
12. Radio Havana, June 29, 1966.
13. Interview of Luben Petkoff, quoted by Radio Havana, December 13 and 20, 1966.
14. Quoted by *La República* (Caracas), July 14, 1966, p. 20.
15. "Tacit Split between the PCV and Castro," *La República* (Caracas), September 3, 1966, p. 20.
16. Carlos Valencia, "The Effectiveness of the Venezuelan CP is not under Discussion," *¿Qué?* (Caracas), September 23, 1966, pp. 6–7, translated in *JPRS*, 5058, 1966.
17. Menendez was described as such in the report of his arrival in Havana, December 20, 1966, in *El Mundo* (Havana), December 21, 1966.

161

18. Radio Havana, December 16, 1966.
19. Radio Havana, December 24 and 31, 1966.
20. Castro quoting AFP bulletin from Caracas, March 9, 1967, Radio Havana, March 14, 1967.
21. Gus Hall and Faria spoke for two hours sometime in August 1966. *The Worker*, September 16, 1966.
22. Oscar Levano, quoted in *Pravda*, July 31, 1966.
23. The only significant exception to this pattern was the article by Guatemalan Communist Bernardo Alvarado Monzon, *WMR*, October 1966, pp. 21–27, and even he conceded that nonviolent forms of struggle will logically predominate in all of Latin America outside the Caribbean area.
24. *Voz Proletaria* (Bogotá), No. 150 (November 3, 1966), pp. 10–11.
25. *Política* (Mexico City), February 14, 1967.

Chapter VIII.

1. Draper, *Castroism, Theory and Practice*, p. 50.
2. The page references in the text are to the Grove Press edition of Regis Debray, *Revolution in the Revolution* (New York, 1967), translated by Bobbye Ortiz. In a few instances, however, the language is from the earlier *JPRS* translation, *JPRS*, 40,310, March 20, 1967, based on a copy of the Cuban text which appeared in *Política* (Mexico City), February 14, 1967.
3. From *JPRS* text, p. 51. The "force of law" phrase is missing from the Grove Press translation.
4. For example, the letter from the PCV to Castro in late August 1966 spoke of "another maneuver by those who have betrayed their condition as military men to usurp positions which they were unqualified to exercise." *La República* (Caracas), September 3, 1966, p. 20.
5. Radio Havana, February 7, 1967.
6. S. S. Mikhailov, "Osnovnya cherty natsional'no-osvoboditel' novo dvizheniya v latinskoi Amerike na sovremennom etape," *Osvoboditel'noe dvizhenie v Latinskoi Amerike* (Moscow: Nauka, 1964), pp. 5–19.
7. "The National-Liberation Movement and Social Progress" (prepared by the Institutes of the Peoples of Asia, Africa, and Latin America of the U.S.S.R. Academy of Sciences), *Kommunist*, No. 13 (1965).
8. *Yuri Arbatov*, "The Building of Socialism in the USSR and the World Revolutionary Process," *Pravda*, September 7, 1966 (emphasis supplied).

9. Carlos Valencia, "The Effectiveness of the Venezuelan CP is not under Discussion," *¿Qué?* (Caracas), September 23, 1966, pp. 6–7.
10. Vitaliy Korionov, in *Pravda*, March 10, 1967.
11. A. Sivolobov, "Different Means, a Common Goal," *Izvestia*, September 24, 1966, p. 2.
12. From *JPRS* text, p. 58.
13. Arbatov, *Pravda*, September 7, 1966, Castro's speech of August 29, 1966, Radio Havana, August 30, 1967.
14. See in particular the Uri Ra'anan, "Moscow and the Third World," *Problems of Communism*, January-February 1965, pp. 22 31.
15. *Bol'shaya Sovetskaya Entsyclopediya*, 1965, p. 231; 1966, p. 236.

BIBLIOGRAPHY

Books

Alexander, Robert J. *Communism in Latin America*. New Brunswick, N.J.: Rutgers University Press, 1957.
Debray, Régis. *Revolution in the Revolution*. Translated by Bobbye Ortiz. New York: Grove Press, 1967.
Dinerstein, Herbert S. *Soviet Policy in Latin America*. Rand Corporation Memorandum RM-4967-PR, May 1966.
Draper, Theodore. *Castro's Revolution: Myths and Realities*. New York: Praeger, 1962.
———. *Castroism: Theory and Practice*. New York: Praeger, 1965.
Guevara, Ernesto "Che." *Guerrilla Warfare*. New York: Monthly Review Press, 1961.
Lockwood, Lee. *Castro's Cuba, Cuba's Fidel*. New York: Macmillan, 1967.
Mikhailov, S. S., ed. *Osvoboditel'noe dvizhenive v Latinskoi Amerike*. Moscow: Nauka, 1964.
Poppino, Rollie E. *International Communism in Latin America*. New York: Macmillan, 1964.

Documents

Council of the Organization of American States. *Report on the First Afro-Asian-Latin American Peoples Solidarity Conference and Its Projections*. 2 vols. Washington: Pan American Union, November 28, 1966.
"Documents of the Venezuelan Communist Movements," *Confidencial* (Caracas), no. 32 (August 1966), pp. 1–55, translated in U.S. Department of Commerce, *Joint Publications Research Service*, 38,275, October 21, 1966.